Once Apun A Time

A Rich, Historical and Sometimes Earthy Collection of Puns

Robin Leech, P.Biol.

Illustrations by
Lorie J. Taylor Leech

 FriesenPress

Suite 300 - 990 Fort St
Victoria, BC, Canada, V8V 3K2
www.friesenpress.com

ISBN
978-1-4602-6887-2 (Hardcover)
978-1-4602-6888-9 (Paperback)
978-1-4602-6889-6 (eBook)

1. Humor

Distributed to the trade by The Ingram Book Company

Table of Contents

DEDICATION

Alwyn Bradley Ewen

24 October 1932 - 25 September 2008

This book is dedicated to Alwyn (Al) Bradley Ewen, aka ABE, entomologist, biologist, scientist, friend, and a former Scientific Editor of *The Canadian Entomologist*. Puns were his favorite humor form.

ACKNOWLEDGEMENTS

Alwyn B. Ewen, Robert C. Cumbow, Merry A. Kogut, Lori Bard Mendel, Hap McGill, Paul McCormack, Dwayne Mills, Steve Duff, Jon W.M. Schorer, Court Atkinson, Pat Berge Muckle, Stephen Thorpe, Dwayne Mills and the late George R. Nock, III, are all graciously thanked. Each has helped with suggestions and contributions, especially during the early stages of preparing this book. We also thank computer whizzes Ethan Wallwork and Andrew Eisenhawer for frequent advice and help on how to prepare special documents. Judith Tomlinson, English grammar maven, proof-reader and friend of many years, is thanked for reviewing the entire manuscript. Lastly, staff at Friesen Press, Victoria, BC, are thanked for nudges to help keep us on line and in line during the preparation of *Once Apun a Time.*

STARTING THIS BOOK

About the year 2000, or perhaps even earlier, I wrote a letter to Al Ewen to see if he were interested in co-authoring a book of puns with me. He was! Even though we no longer had the formal relationship of him being the Scientific Editor of *The Canadian Entomologist* (Nov 1985 to Dec 1993), and of me being one of the Associate Editors (1978 to 2012), we had stayed in rather continuous contact with one another by email, hard copy letter and telephone. We sent many kinds of humor to one another, especially puns, many of which were of our own making.

So puns became the centre-point of our humor exchanges, many of them with comments such as "Tops, eh?", "Keeper!" and "Not so good!" and "What do you think?" attached to them. By default, I became the store house for all the puns we exchanged. About 2004 or 2005, Al purchased a used book of puns on the internet. We each felt that this might be a source for a few more puns, or a source for creating new puns – we both have that twist in our brains that hears the potential or germinal material for a pun, then creates a new pun on the spot.

But, when he received the pun book and read it, he was very disappointed. He never did cite even one of them from this book to me. He felt that they were of too a poor quality to be enjoyed by a dedicated **paronomasiac** (someone addicted to puns and word play), and that our

collection contained many that are a lot better. He must have thrown the book away, as after Al's death, his wife could not find it in his belongings.

Later when fine artist, illustrator and teacher, Lorie Taylor, came into my life, Al, Lorie and I agreed that it would have to be an illustrated book of puns. This in itself would set our book of puns apart from most of the others.

Al died unexpectedly in September 2008 at the age of 75. With his death notice, a message went out to all the entomologists and members of *The Canadian Entomologist* across Canada, asking if any had contributions to make to his obituary notice, which was to be published in December 2008 edition of *The Bulletin of The Canadian Entomologist.*

This triggered me into action to submit two fitting, biological puns for the *Bulletin.* However, at that time, the pun files were scattered in numerous emails to many friends, in WordPerfect files, in Word files, in Humor files, on slips of paper, on both 5.25-inch and 3.5-inch floppy discs, and several other places (only the older folk will recall things such as 5.25-inch and 3.5-inch floppies). A few had even been printed and collected in a loose-leaf binder.

I did find two puns suitable for Al's obituary, and Lorie created illustrations for them. They were published in the *Bull. Ent. Soc. Can.* Vol. **40**(4): 200. They are published here as Bee and Wasp, and Snakes in Noah's Ark.

The sorting, evaluating and printing of the puns in my collection started in earnest in December 2008. Not all

were gathered just by Al and me. Some are originals of our own making, and a few came from friends. A small collection of the puns in this book came to me from a high school graduate classmate, George Nock, III. After his death in 2005, two of his former students, Merry Kogut and Robert Cumbow (both lawyers in the State of Washington, U.S.A.) passed his collection of puns to me with the proviso that there is proper acknowledgement. You will find their names as abbreviations (MAK), (RCC), and (GRN) with the respective puns. RL

PUN HISTORY AND DEFINITIONS

Pun History

Examples of puns can be found in the Bible (Old and New Testaments). One of the better-known ones is found in *Matthew* 16.18:

> "Thou art Peter, and upon this
> rock I will build my church."
>
> (In the Greek text, a play on the word
> "rock" (*petra*) and the name "Peter"
> (*petros*), which also means "stone".)

Puns using the names of pharaohs of Egypt, found in the Biblical literature, have been used to date historical events. William Shakespeare is estimated to have used over 3,000 puns in his plays [Wickipedia. (http://en.wikipedia.org/wiki/Pun)], and puns have been used by well-known writers such as Alexander Pope, James Joyce, John Donne and Lewis Carroll [Webster's Online Dictionary (http://www.websters-online-dictionary.org/definition/pun)], Accessed 7 Feb 2009.

Pun Definitions

Gage Canadian Dictionary

A humorous use of a word in which it can be taken as having two or more different meanings is a play on words. To make puns. First syllable of Italian *puntiglio* means a verbal quibble. Example: *One berry to another: "If you hadn't been so fresh, we wouldn't be in this jam."* 1997. Revised and Expanded. Gage Educational Publishing Company, Toronto.

ITP Nelson Canadian Dictionary of the English Language

A pun is a play on words, sometimes on different senses of the same words and sometimes on the similar sense or sound of different words. To make puns or a pun. 1997. International Thompson Publishing, Scarborough.

Oxford English Dictionary, Compact 2nd Edition

The use of a word in such a way as to suggest two or more meanings or different associations, or the use of two or more words of the same or nearly the same sound with different meanings, so as to produce a humorous effect; a play on words. 1991. Page 1461.

Webster's New International Dictionary, 2nd Edition

Perh. fr. It., *puntiglio*, quibble, fine point. A play on words of the same sound, but different meanings or on different application of a word, with witty or humorous effect; a kind of verbal quibble.

SYN.: PUN, PARONOMASIA, ASONANCE.

A PUN is a play on words of the same sound but different meaning, or on different meanings of the same word, always for the sake of ludicrous effect; PARANOMASIA in rhetoric is a play on words of similar but not the same sound, commonly for antithesis; the word, however, is often synonymous with *pun*. ASSONANCE, as here compared, denotes mere resemblance of a sound without relation to significance. 1954. G. & C. Merriam Co. The Riverside Press, Cambridge, Mass.

Wikipedia, the Free Encyclopedia

A pun or paronomasia is a phrase that deliberately exploits confusion between similar-sounding words for humorous or rhetorical effect. Puns are a form of word play, and can occur in all natural languages. By definition, a pun must be deliberate. An involuntary substitution of similar words is called a malaproprism. (Internet, January 2009)

Etymology

The word *pun* has been used in English since at least the 1600s (Oxford English Dictionary, Compact 2nd edition, 1991, p.1468, "...soon after 1660..."), or possibly even since 1550 (http://en.wikipedia.org/wiki/Pun). It may be a contraction of the now archaic *pundigrion*. This term is thought to have originated from *punctilious,* which is derived from the Italian *puntiglio,* the diminutive of *punto,* "point", from the Latin *punctus,* past participle of *pungere*, "to prick." These are labelled "conjecture" by the OED.

A perfect pun exploits word pairs that sound exactly alike (perfect homophones), or two senses of the same word. For example, "Being in politics is just like playing golf: you are trapped in one bad *lie* after another." And, "When drinking, don't *drive*. Don't even *putt*."

Wikipedia cites an extended pun or pun sequence, which is a long utterance that contains multiple puns with a common theme, to wit:

> "A fight broke out in the kitchen. *Egged* on by the waiters, two cooks *peppered* each other with punches. One man, a *greasy* foie gras specialist, *ducked* the first blows, but his *goose was cooked* when the other *cold-cocked* him. The man who *beet* him, a *weedy* salad expert with big *cauliflower ears*, tried to flee the scene, but was *corner*ed in the *maize* of tables by a *husky* off-duty *cob*. He was charged with *a salt* and *battery*. He claims to look forward to the *suit*, as he's always wanted to be a *sous-chef*."

ABOUT PUNS

Depending on a reader's or listener's experiences, attitudes, perspectives and a few other things regarding puns, puns may be perceived as being **agathokakological.** That is, the Ying and the Yang, or aichmophobic or aichmophilic. In other words, extremes only. No half ways. They are either loved, or treated with contempt. Puns are also most appreciated by those who are alert, have knowledge of history and politics, and as with word mavins, are full of mental energy, and not by those who are tired or drowsy. The reason for this is that puns have several natures and qualities, and belong to those special-fun-with-the-English-language phenomena such as Rebus puzzles, palindromes, anagrams, oxymorons, tongue twisters, etc.

Many puns are fleeting and transitory, devised and stated in a flash for a situation or immediate condition (see Word Plays, and Puns Intended on the Internet), and which may or may not be recoined, resurrected or reinvented by others at later events. It is my contention that many fleeting puns are heard and groaned at immediately, enjoyed, but never heard again. And even if the pun could be recalled, each new situation is different, so reusing the pun will not "work" as it did the first time unless the pun itself is reworked and reworded. These kinds of puns can be retold effectively only if the actual event that triggered it is told in detail in conjunction with the pun.

But some puns are enduring! These can be memorized and told over and over in different social contexts and events, each time with the same overall effects - enjoyed by the teller, and enjoyed by the groaning, appreciative audience. Some of these enduring puns are tongue twisters, so tellers are advised to practice telling them in private so as not to miss any key words along the way that might lessen the effects of the punch line. These kinds of puns can be told independent of any real situation, past or present.

In preparing this book of puns, we examined a number of pun books with the idea in mind of looking for the most suitable arrangement for puns within a book. We were not looking to find puns new to us, as we already had those we wanted. Chapter topics could have included the following: 1-liners; 2-4 liners; 5-10 liners; Groaners; Canadian, USA and British, etc.; Biblical/Religious; Mixed Company; Adult Only; Shakespeare; and many others. But none was found to be satisfactory. It also occurred to us that a section with similar or somehow related puns might lessen the overall pleasure in reading them because of overload. So the only hiving off was for the Salacious/Earthy (read at your own risk) puns. These are at the end of the book.

The punishment for not enjoying puns will be to hear and read them everywhere you go for the rest of your life.

SELECTED PUN BOOKS
FOR REFERENCES

Alexander, J. 2006. The World's Funniest Puns. Crombie Jardine Publishing Ltd. Nonsuch Walk, Cheam, Surrey. SM2 7LG. ISBN: 1-905102-66-6. 160 P.

Lederer, R. 2006. Puns Spoken Here. Illustrations by Ian McLean. Wyrick & Co., an Imprint of Gibbs Smith, Publisher, P.O. Box 667, Layton, UT, 84041. ISBN: 0-941711-79-X. 102 p.

Lederer, R. 2006. Get Thee to a Punnery. Illustrations by Bill Thompson. Wyrick & Co., an imprint of Gibbs Smith, Publisher, P.O. Box 667, Layton, UT, 84041. ISBN: 0-941711-82-X. 174 p.

Moger, A. 1992. The Best Book of Puns. A Citadel Press Book, Carol Publishing Group, NY. ISBN: 0-8065-1097-8. 106 p.

Pollack, J. 2011. The Pun Also Rises. How the humble pun revolutionized language, changed history, and made wordplay more than some antics. Gotham Books, published by Penguin Group (USA) Inc. 375 Hudson St., New York, NY.10014. ISBN: 978-1592-40623-4. 212 p.

Westwood, A. 2011. The Little Book of Puns. Canary Press, an imprint of Omnipress Ltd, UK. ISBN: 978-1-907795-02-2. 160 p., illustrated.

Yale, D.R. 2010. Pun Enchanted Evenings: a treasury of wit, wisdom, chuckles, and belly laughs for language lovers. A Healthy Relationship Press LLC, New York. ISBN: 978-0-9791766-4-7. 101 p.

SELECTED PUBLICATIONS
BY THE AUTHOR

Leech, R. 1994. Word clones, or Ball words, in English usage. George E. Ball Memorial Issue. *The Canad.Ent.* 126(3): 921-923.

Leech, R. 1993/2002. Report writing manual: organization, format and style guide for the Preparation, writing and presentation of reports. 2nd edition. xii+173 p., 8 figs, 4 tables. ISBN: 0-9693845-1-3.

Carbyn, L., R. Leech & G.Ash. 2011. The evolution of biological societies in Alberta. *Canad. Field-Naturalist* **124** 321-329, 3 tables, 1 fig., Appendices A&B.

Leech, R. 2014. Age vs Dilated Pupil Size: factors to consider regarding your eyes and Binoculars used for biological research, birding and hunting. AHEIA Conservation Education Magazine. Fall 2014, pp.22-23, 3 figs.

Once Apun A Time

DANGER.....

The base is under assault!
Take cover immediately!

NaCl
NaOH

MAY THE
4TH BE
WITH YOU

On the Fly

While buzzing along one day, a green bottle fly felt something on his back, so he asked,

"Hey, bug on my back, are you a mite?"

The mite replied, "I mite be."

The fly said, "Stupidest pun I ever heard."

And the mite replied, "What do you expect? I just made it up on the fly."

3

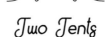

Two Tents

A first-nations chief went to visit a psychiatrist. As he was lying on the couch, the psychiatrist asked him to talk about the stressful things in his life.

The chief said, "When I try to go to sleep, I have these funny feelings that I am a teepee. This will go on for several nights, and then I think I am a wigwam."

"Ahh," said the psychiatrist, "I know your problem. You are too tense."

Painting the Church

A Scot named Wayne MacTavish was a very frugal, thrifty painter. He often thinned the paint with turpentine to make it go a wee bit further.

He got away with this for some time – until the Baptist Church decided to do restorative painting on the outside of one of its biggest buildings. Wayne put in a bid, and because his was the lowest, he got the job.

He set about erecting the scaffolding with the planks, and then bought the paint. And, yes, I am sorry to say, he thinned it with turpentine.

Wayne was up on the scaffolding, painting away, with the job nearly completed. Suddenly there was a horrendous clap of thunder. The sky opened, and the rain poured down, washing all the thinned paint off the church. Wayne was knocked clear off the scaffolding and landed on the lawn among the gravestones. He was surrounded by little puddles of thinned and useless paint.

Wayne was no fool. He knew this was a judgement from the Almighty, so he got down on his knees and cried,

"Oh, God, forgive me! What should I do?"

And from the thunder, a mighty voice spoke,

"Repaint! Repaint and thin no more!"

Whale Meat and Blubber

Recent research has shown that the Inuit who live in small communities eat only whale meat and blubber. The conclusion in the report was that you'd cry, too, if all you had to eat was whale meat.

Wasp Noises

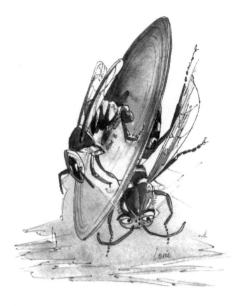

The world's foremost authority on wasps is walking down the street when he sees a record in the window of a charity shop, "Wasp Noises from Around the world." Intrigued, he goes into the shop and asks if he can listen to it.

"Certainly," says the shop assistant and pops it onto his turntable. After listening to the first track for a while, the world's foremost authority on wasps is a bit confused.

"I don't recognize any of these noises, and I'm the world's foremost authority on wasps! Can you play the next track please?"

The assistant obliges and skips the needle onto the next track, but the world's foremost authority on wasps is still confused.

"No, I still don't recognize any of these wasps. Can you try the next track?"

The assistant skips the needle on, and the world's foremost authority on wasps listens for a little while longer before shaking his head. "It's no good. I just don't recognize any of these wasps."

The assistant peers at the label of the record and says...

"Oh, I'm terribly sorry. I had it on the bee side."

Pirate Treasure

A pirate captain was out to retrieve some buried treasure. After a few weeks of sailing, the crew caught sight of land, an island to which his treasure map had been leading him. He and the first mate rowed to the island to search out the treasure, which was supposed to be hidden deep within a swamp at the centre of the island.

Sure enough, at the centre of the island there was a swamp, and the captain and the first mate bravely entered the swamp in their bare feet. The swamp became deeper, and was now just below the knees. At this point, the captain banged his shin on something hard. He reached down, felt around and pulled up a treasure chest.

Pried open, the chest revealed gold and jewels beyond imagination. The captain turned to the first mate and said, "Arrrr, matey, that just goes to show ye that booty is only shin deep!"

Whale Pictures

A man phoned a shop named *The Art Palace*, asking for the address. As it was nearby, he said that he would be there in 10-15 minutes.

When he arrived, he said, "I'm here to pick up the prints of whales!" Without missing a beat, the owner said, "I'm sorry, sir, but you have come to the wrong Palace. Try the big square building in London."

Prayers for Solution

"If there is anyone with 'needs' to be prayed over, please come forward to the front of the alter," the Preacher said.

Several get in line, and when it is Leroy's turn, the Preacher asked, "Leroy, what do you want me to pray about for you?"

Leroy replied, "Preacher, I need you to pray for help with my hearing!"

The Preacher put one finger in Leroy's ear, and the other atop Leroy's head. He then prayed and prayed and prayed. He prayed a blue streak for Leroy, and the whole congregation joined in with enthusiasm.

After a few minutes, the Preacher removed his hands, stood back and asked, "Leroy, how is your hearing now?"

Leroy replied, "I don't know Preacher. It isn't until next Wednesday!"

4 - Word Headline

What four-word headline described the abduction of a crooked pawnbroker, a Mr Wyle of ER, and a female religious?

NOAH, FENCE, NUN TAKEN

Science Friction

Science friction is the conflict that arises between scientists over who will be the lead author on an article they want to publish together.

A Community of Friars

A community of friars was behind on its mortgage payments, so the friars opened a small flower shop to help raise funds. Because everyone felt good about buying flowers from men of God, a rival florist thought the competition had an unfair advantage.

He asked the good friars to close, but they wouldn't. He begged them to close. They ignored him. So, the rival florist hired Hugh MacTaggart, the toughest man in town, to **persuade** the friars to close.

Hugh threatened the friars and trashed their store, saying he'd be back if they didn't close shop. Terrified, they did so, proving that only Hugh can prevent florist friars.

A Dark and Stormy Night

Lost on a rainy night, a nun stumbles across a monastery and requests shelter there. Fortunately, she's just in time for dinner and is treated to the best fish and chips she had ever tasted.

After dinner, she went into the kitchen to thank the chefs. She was met by two of the Brothers. The first one says, "Hello, I am Brother Michael, and this is Brother Charles."

"I'm very pleased to meet you," replies the nun. "I just wanted to thank you for a wonderful dinner. The fish and chips were the best I've ever had. Out of curiosity, who cooked what?"

Brother Charles replied, "Well, I'm the fish friar."

She turned to the other brother and said, "Then you must be...?"

"Yes, I'm afraid so -- I am the Chip Monk."

Carrion

A vulture boards an airplane, carrying two dead raccoons. The stewardess looks at him and says, "I'm sorry, sir, only one carrion allowed per passenger."

A Frog

A frog goes into a bank and approaches the teller. He can see from her nameplate that the teller's name is Patricia Whack.

So he says, "Mrs Whack, I'd like to get a loan to buy a boat and go on a long vacation."

Patti looks at the frog in disbelief and asks how much he wants to borrow.

The frog says $30,000.

The teller asks his name and the frog says that his name is Kermit Jagger, his dad is Mick Jagger, and that it's OK, as he knows the bank manager.

Patti explains that $30,000 is a substantial amount of money and that he will need to secure some collateral against the loan. She asks if he has anything he can use as collateral.

The frog says, "Sure. I have this," and produces a tiny pink porcelain elephant, about half an inch tall, bright pink and perfectly formed.

Very confused, Patti explains that she'll have to consult with the manager and disappears into a back office. She finds the manager and says,

"There's a frog called Kermit Jagger out there who claims to know you and that he wants to borrow $30,000. And he wants to use this as collateral." She holds up the tiny pink elephant.

"I mean, what the heck is this?" she asks

The bank manager looks back at her and says:

"It's a knickknack, Patti Whack. Give the frog a loan. His old man's a Rolling Stone."

When Pigs Fly

Back in the 1940s in the U.S., when the question came up about a black ever being President of the U.S., the usual retort was, "Yeah, when pigs fly!"

There is now a black president in the Oval Office in Washington, and wouldn't you know it, the swine flu.

Which Service?

One Sunday morning the Reverend noticed little Alex in the foyer of the church, staring up at a large plaque. It was

covered with names with small Canadian flags mounted on either side of it.

The seven-year-old had been staring at the plaque for some time, so the Reverend walked over, stood beside the little boy and said quietly,

"Good morning, Alex,"

"Good morning, Reverend," he replied, still focussed on the plaque.

"Reverend, what is this?" he asked.

The Reverend replied, "Well, son, it's a memorial to all the young men and women who died in the service."

Soberly, they just stood together, staring at the large plaque.

Finally, little Alex's voice, barely audible and trembling with fear, asked,

"Which service? The 8:00 or the 10:30 a.m.?"

A Fryer

Two cannibals were good friends. One went over to visit with his buddy and found him on the ground, rolling and groaning something fierce. He was obviously in serious trouble.

"Hey, man, what's the problem?" asked the visitor.

"Groan! Ate a missionary. Ohhhhh!"

"Yeah, yeah," said the visitor. "How did you cook him?"

"Ohhh, first I boiled him. Still tough, so I roasted him. Still tough! Ohhhh."

"What did he look like?" asked the visitor.

"Ohhh, big heavy guy. Big brown robe with a sash. Bald on top with a bit of hair around the fringes. Ohhh."

"Ohh, boy!" exclaimed the visitor. "No wonder you're in pain and agony. That was a friar."

A Man and His Pet

A travelling salesman was tired of coming home after a long hard day to an empty house. He was single, as in his profession, he rarely met women. And as he was away all day for six days per week, he felt he could not have a pet and take care of it. Late one evening after supper, he was watching the TV, and a pet shop was advertising that it had a few new pets, among them a small rodent called a rarie. Raries come from the boggy parts of central Ireland, and are about the size of a house cat. They have no tail to speak of -- just a little stump, much like that of a guinea pig.

The advertising blurb said that raries can pretty well take care of themselves, and that they would be ideal for someone who was not home all day. Further, it was said that raries are very cuddly and when one comes home at night, a rarie will greet you at the door like a long-lost lover. Raries make all sorts of sounds, indicating pleasure, needing to be held, wanting to go for a walk, wanting more food in the food dish, and other sounds to indicate needs.

So, he went to the pet shop on his day off. He grilled the pet shop owner about the habits of the rarie, how much food it needed, did it need special foods, places for it to go potty, how long it might live, how clean they are, and so on. He was satisfied with the answers, so he purchased a rarie, along with all the food dishes, foods, potty and potty litter, etc. And it didn't cost him a fortune, so he was very happy.

Every night when he came home, he was greeted at the door by his pet rarie, and over a number of years, he and the rarie became very close.

Then one day when he came home, he noted a change in the rarie. It had grown a little bit. Over the next few weeks, he noted more growth. When the rarie became the size of a German shepherd, he began to worry, not so much because of the extra food required, but there wasn't all that much space in his small home. He went back to the pet shop and asked the owner about the growing problem. The owner had never heard of this before. So the man checked on the Internet and found that 1 in 200,000 raries has the growth problem, and that they continue to grow.

A few weeks later, the rarie was the size of a bear, and shortly after that, it was big enough that it was causing the floor to sink down, as it took up most of the living room. It was now also too large to get out the door. He made the decision: the rarie had to go.

He rented a large dump truck, and backed up against the house. He then cut a huge hole in the wall of the living room, rolled the rarie onto the dump truck. He drove the truck up a local mountain, and at the highest viewpoint, he backed the dump truck up to the edge of the steep slope. He then pushed the lever to tip up the dumper. In short order, the rarie was tipped off the dump truck. As he watched his dear, beloved rarie bounce down the steep slope, he thought to himself, "It's a long way to tip a rarie."

Peaches

The minister of a city church enjoyed a drink now and then, but his passion was for peach brandy. One of his congregation members would make him a bottle each Christmas.

One year, when the minister went to visit his friend, hoping for his usual Christmas present, he was not disappointed. But his friend told him that had to thank him for the peach brandy from the pulpit the next Sunday. In his haste to get the bottle, the minister hurriedly agreed and left.

So the next Sunday the minister suddenly remembered that he had to make a public announcement that he was being supplied alcohol from a member of the church. That morning, his friend sat in the church with a grin on his face, waiting to see the minister's embarrassment.

The minister climbed into the pulpit and said, "Before we begin, I have an announcement. I would like to thank my friend, Joe, for his kind gift of peaches … and for the spirit in which they were given!"

Worker Bee

A worker bee went into a bank to get a job application, and to see about getting a job. However, the teller tried to get the bee to open a chequing account first, suggesting to the bee that once she had a chequing account, she could apply for a loan.

The bee replied, "Look, I am a worker bee. I'm neither a lender nor a borrower bee."

Yewin

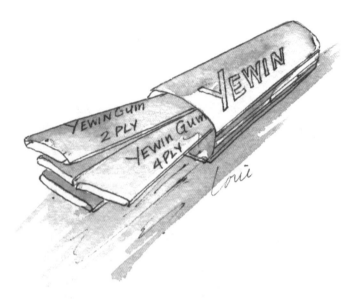

Two men were in the process of inventing a new brand of gum. They were arguing over the fact that their new gum was too hard and brittle, and did not have the right consistency.

One of the inventors kept arguing that they simply had to add more liquid to their primary secret ingredient, code named "Yewin."

The other man argued adamantly, "No, no. NO!! It's not wetter Yewin that counts . . . it's how you ply the gum.

Pi (π)

I asked my English teacher a question about pi (π), but her answer was never-ending.

Pupil Control

Dr Jim Jones was a brilliant mathematician. He received his BSc when he was 16, and his PhD when he was 20. He worked in industry for a while, but he really wanted to teach, so he applied to a university. The faculty knew his academic history, so they were delighted to bring him on board.

But he had a severe physical problem with his eyes: when he looked at you, his eyes would cross instantly and stay that way. This upset the other faculty and really disturbed the students, who became unruly in the classrooms.

The university let him go on the grounds that he could not control his pupils.

One - Liner Puns (Mostly)

Energizer Bunny arrested - charged with battery.

A man's home is his castle, in a manor of speaking.

A pessimist's blood type is always B-negative.

A pun is its own best reword.

My wife really likes to make pottery, but to me it's just kiln time.

Dijon vu - the same mustard as before.

The short fortune teller who escaped from prison is now a small medium at large.

Practice safe eating - always use condiments.

I fired my masseuse today. She just rubbed me the wrong way.

A Freudian slip is when you say one thing but mean your mother.

Shotgun wedding: A case of wife or death.

I used to work in a blanket factory, but it folded.

I used to be a lumberjack, but I just couldn't hack it, so they gave me the axe.

If electricity comes from electrons... does that mean that morality comes from morons?

Marriage is the mourning after the knot before.

A hangover is the wrath of grapes.

Corduroy pillows are making headlines.

Sea captains don't like crew cuts.

Does the name Pavlov ring a bell?

A gossip is someone with a great sense of rumor.

Without geometry, life is pointless.

When you dream in color, it's a pigment of your imagination.

Reading whilst sunbathing makes you well-red.

Honeymoon salad: lettuce alone with very little dressing.

When two egotists meet, it's an I for an I.

"I am" is the shortest sentence in the English language.

"I do" is the longest sentence in the English language.

If you cannot be an athlete, at least be an athletic supporter.

Two fish swim into a concrete wall. One turned to the other and says, "Dam!"

If at first you don't succeed . . . don't try parachuting or skydiving.

Bagpipes should be played tenor maybe 11 miles away.

A bicycle can't stand alone because it is two-tired.

What's the definition of a will? (It's a dead giveaway.)

Show me a piano falling down a mineshaft and I'll show you A-flat minor.

Any person who commits suicide by jumping off a bridge in Paris is in Seine.

Khaki is what you need to start a car in Boston. (in Canada, we often pronounce this as karkey, so it works with other accents!)

Pasteurize: too far too see.

Toboggan: Why we go to an auction.

Oboe: An English tramp.

Alarms: what an octopus is.

Dockyard: A physician's garden.

Incongruous: Where bills are passed.

Those who groan when they hear puns – are they children or groan-ups?

When I went to the opera, I heard the soprano sing PMS-imo. (GRN)

The roundest knight at King Arthur's round table was Sir Cumference. He acquired his size from too much pi.

I thought I saw an eye doctor on an Alaskan island, but it turned out to be an optical Aleutian.

She was only a whisky-maker, but he loved her still.

A rubber band pistol was confiscated from algebra class because it was a weapon of math disruption.

The butcher backed into the meat grinder and got a little behind in his work.

No matter how much you push the envelope, it'll still be stationery.

A dog gave birth to puppies near the road and was cited for littering.

A grenade thrown into a kitchen in France would result in Linoleum Blownapart.

Two silk worms had a race. They ended up in a tie.

Time flies like an arrow. Fruit flies like a banana.

Atheism is a non-prophet organization.

Two hats were hanging on a hat rack in the hallway. One hat said to the other, 'You stay here. I'll go on a head.'

A sign on the lawn at a drug rehab center said: "Keep off the Grass."

A chicken crossing the road is poultry in motion.

The man who survived mustard gas and pepper spray is now a seasoned veteran.

A backward poet writes inverse.

In democracy it's your vote that counts. In feudalism it's your count that votes.

When cannibals ate a missionary, they got a taste of religion.

Local Area Network in Australia: the LAN down under.

He often broke into song because he couldn't find the keys.

Every calendar's days are numbered.

A lot of money is tainted. It taint yours and it taint mine.

A boiled egg in the morning is hard to beat.

A plateau is a high form of flattery.

Those who get too big for their britches will be exposed in the end.

When an actress saw her first strands of gray hair, she thought she'd dye.

Bakers trade bread recipes on a knead-to-know basis.

Santa's helpers are subordinate clauses.

Acupuncture is a jab well done.

Jokes about German sausages are the wurst.

When you get a bladder infection, you know urine trouble.

I got a job in a bakery because I kneaded dough.

Marathon runners with bad footwear suffer the agony of defeat.

She had a relationship with a boyfriend with a wooden leg, but she broke it off.

If you don't pay your exorcist, you will be repossessed.

The man who fell into the upholstery machine is fully recovered.

You feel stuck with your budget if you can't budge it.

Palindromes work back words.

Walletting is a word that begins and ends with letting.

I tried to be a chef, figuring it would add a little spice to my life, but I just didn't have the thyme.

Then I was a professional fisherman, but I found that I couldn't live on my net income.

For a while, I worked for a pool maintenance company, but the work was just too draining.

My last job was working at Starbucks, but I had to quit because it was always the same old grind.

Does a male chauvinist pig have swine empathy?

He's not a bad dancer – he's just overly Caucasian.

Some think he gets lost all the time, but he is really checking out alternative destinations.

He is not balding. He is in hair follicle regression.

Two Eskimos in a kayak were chilly, so they started a fire, which caused the kayak to sink. This proved the old adage, "You can't have your kayak and heat it too."

I went to the butcher's the other day and bet him $50 that he couldn't reach the meat off the top shelf. He said, "No thanks, the steaks are too high."

With her marriage, she got a new name and a dress.

Fly Fishing

It was a beautiful day, and the fisherman had come from afar to fly fish in this particular stream. The stream alternated between gentle rapids and large, deep pools - pools of clear, cool water, just perfect for fly-fishing for trout. Not far from where he stood, he could see large carp sampling the detritus on the bottom of the pond.

As the fisherman stood there in his hip waders, assessing this particular pool, a beautiful fish leaped out of the water to catch a caddisfly. A moment later, another fish leaped to catch a mayfly. Excitedly, he checked his stash of tied flies, looking first at the Grey Dunn, but then selected a Royal Coachman, and tied the fly to the long leader.

As he flicked his wrist back and forth with false casts, and as the line moved smoothly in increasingly long loops in the air, he fed the line through the eyelets of his long, split cane fly rod. On the third flick he cast, and the fly landed about a metre from where the last fish had leaped, leaving a long line trail on the surface. He quickly pulled the line and fly along the surface with his right hand, and prepared for another cast with his left.

On his second cast, as the fly whipped by him, it caught the wallet in his back pocket and flung it out to where the fish were jumping. Just as the wallet hit the water, one of the large carp came to the surface and hit the wallet with its mouth, bouncing the wallet about a half-metre into the air. And as the wallet hit the water, a second carp hit the wallet, and again the wallet went flying. For about 15 second, he saw three large carp bouncing his wallet among them. Then it sank.

The fly fisherman was astounded. He had read of this kind of thing happening, but had never seen it. In the fishing literature, it is known as carp-to-carp walletting.

Flying School

I have been thinking of opening a flying school:

1. 20 weeks for the complete course.

2. 20 hours for the crash course.

McDonald's Restaurant

Two frogs drove up to the drive-in part of a McDonald's Restaurant.

The voice on the intercom asked, "May I take your order, please?"

The driver said, "Yes, two hamburgers and two cokes, please!"

The voice on the intercom asked, "Do you want flies with that?"

Chicken Surprise

A couple went to a Chinese restaurant to order the "Chicken Surprise". A little later, the waiter brought the meal, served in a lidded cast-iron pot. Just as the wife is about to serve herself, the lid of the pot rises slightly, and she briefly sees two beady little eyes looking around before the lid slammed down. "Good grief, did you see that?" she asked her husband.

He didn't so she asks him to look into the pot. He reached for the pot just as the lid rises again, and he saw two little eyes looking around before the lid slammed. Rather perturbed, he called the waiter over, and explained what happened, and demanded an explanation.

"Please, sir," asked the waiter, "what did you order?"

The husband replied, "Chicken Surprise."

"Ah . . . so sorry," said the waiter. "I brought you Peeking Duck."

California Pinot Wines

A California vintner in the Napa Valley area that produces Pinot blanc and Pinot Grigio wines has developed a new hybrid grape that acts as an anti-diuretic and promises to reduce the number of trips an older person has to make to the bathroom during the night.

They will be marketing the new wine as Pinot More.

Historians Are Wondering

Historians are wondering if General George Custer was wearing an Arrow shirt during his final battle.

Help from Ottawa

A man dressed very neatly in a suit and tie, with polished black shoes, came into a small business store in Alberta.

The owner looked the man over and asked, "What may I do for you?"

The man in the suit replied, "I work with the federal government. I've been sent to help you!"

House Calls

A woman was married to a medical doctor. He frequented a particular gambling house in Edmonton, and was well

known there. She called the gambling house, saying it was an emergency, and that she had to speak to her husband.

The receptionist said, "I am sorry, Ma'am. The house does not make doctor calls."

Pythagoras 's Theorem

Three first-Nations women are sitting on the ground facing one another. The first woman is sitting on a bison hide and her son weighs 55 kg. The second woman is sitting on a deer hide and her son weighs 45 kg. The third woman is sitting on a hippopotamus hide and her son weighs 100 kg.

Pythagoras's Theorum Proved: the weight of the sons of the squaws on the two hides is equal to the weight of the son of the squaw on the hippopotamus hide.

Quiet Watch in Macedonia

Outside a small Macedonian village, a lone Catholic nun keeps a quiet watch over a silent convent. She is the last caretaker of this site of significant historical developments, spanning more than 2,000 years.

When Sister Maria Cyrilla of the Order of the Perpetual Watch dies, the convent of St Elias will be closed by the Eastern Orthodox Patriarch of Macedonia. However, that isn't likely to happen soon, as Sister Maria, 53, enjoys excellent health. By her own estimate, she walks 10 miles daily about the grounds of the convent, which once served as a base for the army of Attila the Hun.

In more ancient times, a Greek temple to Eros, the god of love, occupied the hilltop site. Historians say that Attila took over the old temple in 439 A.D., and used it as a base for his marauding army. The Huns are believed to have first collected and then destroyed a large gathering of Greek legal writs at the site. It is believed that Attila wanted to study the Greek legal system and had the writs and other documents brought to the temple.

Scholars differ on why he had the valuable documents destroyed. It could be because he was barely literate and couldn't read them, or because they provided evidence of a democratic government that did not square with his own notion of "rule by an all-powerful tyrant."

When the Greek Church took over the site in the 15th century and the convent was built, church leaders ordered the pagan statue of Eros destroyed, causing yet another ancient Greek treasure to be lost. Today, there is only the lone sister, watching over the old Hun base. When she goes, that will be it.

Thus, that's how it ends, with No Huns, No Writs, and No Eros.

Simon Fraser 's Ears

Q: How many ears did Simon Fraser, the explorer of western Canada, have?

A: Three. A left ear; a right ear; and the Western frontier.

Sir Edgbert

Sir Edgbert, knight of the realm, was hurrying home on a cold, dark, wet night when, suddenly, his horse suffered a major coronary and died on the spot. All Sir Edgbert could do was collect up what belongings he could and tramp onwards.

After staggering for a spell, he decided that he must get alternative transport. Accordingly, he headed for the nearest building which, as luck would have it, was a small farm. He strode up to the door, banged on it and shouted, "A horse! A horse!. I must have a horse!"

The door opened to reveal a young girl. She looks at Sir Edgbert and said, "Your pardon, Good Knight, but my father and brothers are returning from the village on the other side of the forest and will not be back before noon tomorrow. They are riding all our horses".

Sir Edgbert is saddened by this and says, "But I must return home immediately. Have you any idea where I may acquire alternative transportation?"

The young girl says, "I know of no other horses hereabouts, but sometimes my brothers ride our Great Dane dog when the need arises. Would use of that help?"

Sir Edgbert is desperate and said "If I must, I must. Show me the animal". The young girl led the way around to the back of the farmhouse to a stable. She disappeared inside and returned, leading an enormous dog which is quite of a size for riding. Unfortunately, the dog has seen better days. Its coat is threadbare, its legs are spindly and it seems to be breathing laboriously.

Sir Edgbert looks at the young girl and asked, "Surely, you wouldn't send a knight out on a dog like this?"

Faizal the Lemur

There was once a lemur called Faizal. Faizal was no ordinary lemur. In fact, instead of wasting his time sitting around with the other lemurs, Faizal would spend his days and nights drinking at the local pub. Faizal became a legend. He would sit at the bar and tell stories of lemur legend while everybody bought him drinks.

Unfortunately, our friend Faizal had a bit of a temper, and became involved in a horrible dispute one night. One thing led to another, and Faizal was horribly dismembered by a young lout with a flicknife. His bloodied corpse lay on the pavement outside the pub, and his severed fluffy tail lay in the gutter. He was pronounced dead at the scene.

So disheartened were the pub's patrons that they commissioned a plaque in Faizal's honor. They had his cute fluffy tale mounted to a mahogany plaque, which they hung above the bar. One Sunday evening after closing time, there was a knock on the pub door. The bartender opened the door, and who should be there but a ghostly possessed visage of the deceased Faizal.

"Holy mother of Jesus," said the barman, "it's Faizal".

The ghost lifted a ghostly finger and pointed towards the plaque above the bar, and then towards his own ghostly severed stump where a tail should have been.

"Ahhh", said the barman, "you want your tail back, don't you?"

The ghostly lemur nodded.

"Sorry," said the barman, "but we don't retail spirits on a Sunday".

In Sync, In June, In Time

The newly hired musician was having trouble keeping the beat with the rest of the cruise ship's orchestra.

Finally, the captain, in desperation, threatened: "Either you learn to keep up, or I will throw you overboard! It's up to you to sync or swim."

Late One Foggy Night

A man is walking home alone late one foggy night, when behind him he hears sound he cannot identify. So he starts walking a bit faster, and when he looks back over his shoulder, he sees an upright casket banging its way down the middle of the street towards him.

Now terrified, he begins to run home, and the casket increases its speed, too. Up the front walk to the steps, jams the key into the lock, opens the door, rushes in, and slams and locks the door behind himself.

The casket crashes through the door, the lid clapping loudly. He runs upstairs to the bathroom and locks himself in. The casket crashes through the bathroom door, clapping as it goes toward him.

The man screams, reaches for something, anything, but all he can find is a bottle of cough syrup, which in desperation, he throws at the casket. As the bottle smashes, the coffin stops.

Geek

A friend of mine is a computer geek, and is really fast on the keyboard. He brought this speed from the computer to the TV remote, and frequently flipped channels at incredible speeds.

He was busy doing this one evening, when his new wife said, "Hon, I wish you wouldn't do that, it really irks me."

He then slowed his channel flipping, and this mollified her a bit, but he started to whistle. This really got to her, so she asked, "Just what is it you think you are doing?"

He replied, "I'm whistling while I irk."

Golf Gun

Two Mexican detectives were investigating the murder of Juan Gonzalez. "How was he killed?" asked one detective. "With a golf gun," the other detective replied. "A golf gun? What's a golf gun?" "I don't know, but it sure made a hole in Juan."

The Hills are Alive

Bob Hill and his new wife, Betty, were honeymoon-vacationing in Europe, as it happened in Transylvania. They were driving a rental car along a rather deserted highway. It was late, and raining very hard. Bob could barely see 3 metres in front of the car. Suddenly the car skidded out of control! Bob attempted to control the car, but to no avail! The car swerved and smashed into a tree. Moments later, Bob shook his head to clear the fog. Dazed, he looked over at the passenger seat and saw his new wife, unconscious, with her head bleeding! Despite the rain and unfamiliar countryside, Bob knew he had to carry her to the nearest phone. Bob carefully picked up his wife and began trudging down the road. After a short while, he saw a light. He headed towards the light, which was coming from an old, large house. He approached the door and knocked.

A minute passed. A small, hunched man opened the door.

Bob immediately blurted, "Hello, my name is Bob Hill, and this is my wife, Betty. We've been hurt. May I please use your phone??"

"I'm sorry," replied the hunchback, "but we don't have a phone. My master is a doctor. Come in and I will get him." Bob brought his wife in. An elegant man came down the stairs.

"I'm afraid my assistant may have misled you. I am not a medical doctor. I am a scientist. However, it is many miles to the nearest clinic, and I have had basic medical training. I will see what I can do. Igor was asked to bring them down to the laboratory."

With that, Igor picked up Betty and carried her downstairs, as Bob followed closely. Igor placed Betty on a table in the lab. Bob collapsed from exhaustion and his own injuries; so Igor placed Bob on an adjoining table. After a brief examination, Igor's master looked worried.

"Things are serious, Igor. Prepare a transfusion." Igor and his master worked feverishly, but to no avail. Bob and Betty Hill are no more. The Hills' deaths upset Igor's master greatly. Wearily, he climbed the steps to his conservatory, which houses his pipe organ. For it is here that he has always found solace. He began to play, and a stirring, almost haunting melody filled the house.

Meanwhile, Igor was still in the lab tidying up. As the music filled the lab, his eyes caught a movement, and he noticed that the fingers on Betty Hill's hand twitched. Stunned, he watched as Bob's arm began to rise! He was further amazed as Betty sat straight up! Unable to contain himself, he dashed up the stairs to the conservatory. He burst in and shouted to his master:

"Master! Master! . . . The Hills are alive with the sound of music!"

A Salt

Two snails were discussing personal defense. One of them showed the other the large can of salt he had handy to protect his family. He further mentioned that there is a safety that keeps the lid on the can. When he saw the concern on his friend's face, he added,

"I realize that a salt is a deadly weapon, so I always keep the safety on."

A Smart Horse

There was once a very smart horse. Anything that was shown it, it mastered easily, until one day, its teachers tried to teach it about rectangular coordinates, and it couldn't understand them. All the horse's acquaintances and friends tried to figure out what was the matter and couldn't. Then a new guy (what the heck, a computer engineer) looked at the problem and said,

"Of course he can't do it. You're putting Descartes before the horse!"

Indian Chief

An Indian Chief was feeling sick, so he summoned the medicine man. After a brief examination, the medicine man took out a long thin strip of elk hide and gave it to the Chief saying, "Bite off a piece of this each day, chew it well and swallow it."

A month later, the medicine man returned to see how the Chief was feeling.

The Chief shrugged, "The thong is ended, but the malady lingers on."

Moon Mining

A group of astronauts is on the moon. They've been mining the surface, and have discovered that it really is made of cheese. One particular area of cheese that they're quite interested in is a large vein of brie, and they've already been there twice, and collected samples to be returned to mission control. All of a sudden, the radio crackles into life: "Mission control to cheese-base-one, we need you to get a third load of that brie!" But the astronauts are unhappy with the idea. They try to come up with all sorts of excuses why they shouldn't dig any more... "It'll spoil the environment if we take too much. We don't want to leave this place looking bad. "After all, have you ever seen such a site in your life as brie mined thrice?"

Aid and Abet Punster's Day

The people who founded this day claim that this is the all-time greatest triple pun:

"Though he's not very humble, there's no police like Holmes."

Afraid Not

Three strings wanting a beer entered a pub one night and sat at the bar. Finally the barkeep came by, took one look at them and said, "Look, we don't serve strings in this pub! Take a hike."

So, they left. Outside they discussed a strategy. One said, "I know, I will tie a knot, then fluff the end. If he doesn't recognized me as a string, then you two tie a knot, too." It was agreed.

The string with the knot and fluffed end sat at the bar. The barkeep looked and asked, "Say, aren't you one of those strings I just kicked out of here?"

The string replied, "No, I'm a frayed knot."

A Grazing Mace

There was once a handyman who had a dog named Mace. Mace was a great dog except he had one weird habit: he liked to eat grass - not just a little bit, but in quantities that would make a lawnmower blush. And nothing, it seemed, could cure him of it.

One day, the handyman lost his wrench in the tall grass while he was working outside. He looked and looked, but it was nowhere to be found. As it was getting dark, he gave up for the night and decided to look the next morning. When he awoke, he went outside, and saw that his dog had eaten the grass all in the area, around where he had been working, and his wrench now lay in plain sight, glinting in the sun.

Going out to get his wrench, he called the dog over to him and said, "A grazing Mace, how sweet the hound, that saved a wrench for me."

Snakes in Noah's Ark

When Noah built his ark, he had two snakes aboard. When the animals were leaving, he said, "Go forth and multiply." The snakes didn't move. "Go forth and multiply!" They still didn't move. Noah was yelling by now. "Go forth and multiply!"

"We can't," they answered. Noah was confused and angry. "And just why not?"

"Because we're adders," they replied.

Definitions for Pun Types:
(17 puns)

Adult:
A person who has stopped growing at both ends and is now growing in the middle.

Beauty Parlor:
A place where women curl up and dye.

Cannibal:
Someone who is fed up with people.

Chickens:
The only animals you eat before they are born and after they are dead.

Committee:
A body that keeps minutes and wastes hours.

Dust:
Mud with the juice squeezed out.

Egotist:
Someone who is usually me-deep in conversation.

Handkerchief:
Cold storage.

Inflation:
Cutting money in half without damaging the paper.

Mosquito:
An insect that makes you like flies better.

Raisin:
Grape with a sunburn.

Secret:
Something you tell to one person at a time.

Skeleton:
A bunch of bones with the person scraped off.

Toothache:
The pain that drives you to extraction.

Tomorrow:
One of the greatest labor saving devices of today.

Yawn:
An honest opinion openly expressed.

Wrinkles:
Something other people have. You have character lines.

No Place Like Home

This guy goes into his dentist's office, because something is wrong with his mouth. After a brief examination, the dentist exclaims:

"Holy Smoke! That plate I installed in your mouth about six months ago has nearly completely corroded! What on earth have you been eating?"

"Well... the only thing I can think of is this... my wife made me some asparagus about four months ago with this stuff on it... Hollandaise sauce she called it... and doctor, I'm talkin' DELICIOUS! I've never tasted anything like it, and ever since then I've been putting it on everything... meat, fish, toast, vegetables... you name it!"

"That's probably it," replied the dentist.

"Hollandaise sauce is made with lemon juice, which is acidic and highly corrosive. It seems as though I'll have to install a new plate, but made out of chrome this time."

"Why chrome?" the man asked ... (are you ready for this???)

"Well, everyone knows that there's no plate like chrome for the Hollandaise!"

Martha Stewart

The investigation of Martha Stewart continues. Her recipe for chicken casserole is quite efficient. First you boil the chicken in water. Then you dump the stock.

Driving Ambition

No one has more driving ambition than the boy who wants to buy a car.

English Mills

At one time, economic conditions caused the closing of several small clothing mills in the English countryside. A man from West Germany bought the buildings and converted them into dog kennels for the convenience of German tourists who liked to have their pets with them while vacationing in England.

One summer evening, a local resident called to his wife to come out of the house.

"Just listen!" he urged. "The Mills Are Alive With the Hounds of Munich!"

Lunchpack

I was visiting France, and while in Paris I decided to take a guided tour around the beautiful cathedral on the banks of the Seine. As we were being shown around the building, I spotted a sandwich box lying on the floor.

So I picked it up, and handed it to the guide. He was very apologetic, and hurried off with it. After a few minutes, I could hear him calling up the bell tower:

"Quazimodo! You left your sandwich box lying around again!"

When the guide returned, he apologized again, and when we asked him about the sandwiches, he said: "Don't worry about it... it's just the Lunchpack of Notre Dame.

March Prophecy

Visiting my ophthalmologist today, she remarked that last year I saw her on March 14, this year on March 16. I told her that I didn't come on March 15, in view of the prophecy "Beware the eye doctors of March." (GRN)

Die Walküre

Hope you enjoyed *Die Walküre.* I will always identify the opera with the Fifties cartoon in which Elmer Fudd sings "Kill the wabbit, kill the wabbit" to the tune of the Ride of the Valkyries. Has a nice Ring to it. (GRN)

Numbered Days

There was a symposium in Switzerland of all horologists, watch makers and repairers, clock makers and repairers, parts makers, the works. Major issues under discussion were time clocks and watches with mechanical works, electronic works, digital and analog readouts.

At the end of the symposium, there was complete agreement that the days of digital watches are numbered .

The Lesser of Two Weevils

There are many species of weevils where I live. The strawberry root weevil and the pine root weevil are two of the most common. As the strawberry root weevil is very much smaller than is the pine root weevil, it is known as the lesser of two weevils.

The Evil of Two Lessers

In a small community, two men ran for mayor. Everyone who knows them knows that both are crooks, and that their social standings in the community are not good. Both candidates are about five feet tall. But one of them was far more devious than the other in the election - he stuffed ballot boxes to ensure a win for himself. He is definitely the more evil of two lessers.

Origin of Independence Day

Do you remember the old joke, that Canadians do not have July 4 – they go directly from the third to the fifth?

Persons attending the Indianapolis 500 on Memorial Day are allowed to order medals featuring the name of the winner, and designed to be worn on a chain around the neck. They are delivered by special messenger on the following July 4. That is why July 4 is called Indy Pendants Day.

Alligator Medicine

There were two alligators, Pete and Tom, who grew up together in the Florida swamps. They were more successful that most at catching prey for food because they worked together - one of them would chase, the other would hide and ambush. They did this for many years.

One day Tom said to Pete, "Hey, I notice that you don't seem to have the speed at chasing you used to have. What's up?" "I dunno," replied Pete. "I think I will go see a vet."

Pete went to the vet, and after extensive tests, the vet handed Pete a few small pills. "What are these for?" asked Pete. The vet replied that they are kind of like Viagra or Cialis.

Pete replied, protesting, "Hey, I don't have that kind of problem. What's wrong with me, anyway?" The vet replied, "You have reptile dysfunction."

Japanapple Choir

It was visitor's day at the lunatic asylum. All the inmates were standing in the courtyard and singing "Ave Maria." They were singing it beautifully.

Oddly, each of them was holding a red apple in one hand and tapping it rhythmically with a pencil. A visitor listened in wonder to the performance, and then approached the conductor.

"I'm a retired choir director," he said. "This is one of the BEST choirs I have ever heard!"

"Yes, I am very proud of them," said the conductor.

"You should take them on tour," said the visitor. "What are they called?"

"Surely that's obvious...," replied the conductor.

"They're the Moron Tapanapple Choir."

That's Odd

The parents of a new baby could not decide what to name their son, so they took the first letters of the names of three of their favorite relatives, Oscar, Dianne and David, and named their son, "Odd."

Decades passed, and after a lifetime of enduring jokes and teasing about his name, poor Odd passed away. He made only one request for his burial arrangements: he did not want his embarrassing name on his tombstone under any circumstances.

Surprisingly, the omission has caused few identification problems. To this day, nearly everyone who notices the tombstone with no name remarks, "Isn't that odd?"

The Rudolph Song

Once upon a time there was a king in Lapland called Rudolph. He had bright ginger hair, so his people called him Rudolph the Red. Now Rudolph the Red was bad-tempered and argued a lot. He gave his poor wife, Gertrude the Green, a terrible time. No matter what she said, he had to argue.

One winter's day Gertrude the Green looked out of the palace window and said, "Oh dear, it's snowing again. You'll have to clear the footpath before mother comes to tea."

"Humph!" Rudolph the Red grunted. He didn't fancy shifting snow, and he didn't want Gertrude the Green's mother coming to tea.

"That's not snow. It's rain!" he argued.

"But it's white and fluffy and drifting," Gertrude the Green tried to tell him.

Rudolph the Red hid behind his newspaper and snapped, "It's rain!"

Gertrude the Green became quite angry. "Gertrude the Green knows snow, darling!"

"Yes," retorted her husband. "And Rudolph the Red knows rain, dear!"

"What a great title for a song!" Gertrude the Green exclaimed.

Baskin' Robins

They flew to the ground and found a nice plot of plowed ground full of worms. They ate and ate and ate 'til they could eat no more.

"I'm so full I don't think I can fly back up to the tree," said the first one. "Me neither! Let's just lie here and bask in the warm sun," said the second. "OK," said the first.

They plopped down, basking in the sun. No sooner had they had fallen asleep when a big fat tomcat snuck up and gobbled them up. As he sat washing his face after his meal, he thought, "I love baskin' robins."

Antique Tents

Once a year, the collectors of antique tents in Germany get together for a rally. Last year, the organizers decided to hold it in Meinz. Unfortunately, the local burghers took a dim view of so great an influx of tourists ruining their turf with tent pegs. The citizens opposed to the rally organized themselves so efficiently that they even had an anthem: . . .

"Let Old and Quaint Tents Be Forgot and Never Brought to Meinz!"

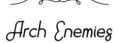

Arch Enemies

Two good friends decided to open a shoe and boot store. Business was super, and in short order they decided that they needed to expand their facility.

A store came up for rent across the street, so it was decided that one would go to the new store, but not carry the lines of shoes and boots that the original store had. This worked out fine for a while, but when the new store with the new lines of shoes and boots started to do a lot more business than the old store, things became unfriendly, and these two long-time friends became arch enemies.

Art Shop

A marine biologist made a phone order to a store called *The Art Palace* for some prints. Later that day he went to *The Art Palace* to pick them up and said to the clerk, "I'm here to pick up the prints of whales."

Without missing a beat, the clerk said, "I'm sorry, sir, but you've come to the wrong Palace! The Prince of Wales lives in the big square building in London!"

After this bit of confusion, the biologist was told that the prints were still in the process of having the colors added. He was then asked, "Do you want to help the lady dye the prints of whales?"

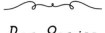

Bar Service

An atom said to another, "I think I just lost an electron!"

"Are you sure?" the other asked.

"I'm positive!"

Be On The Alert!!

A Niagara man was found dead in his home over the weekend. Detectives at the scene found the man face down in his bathtub. The tub had been filled with milk, sugar and cornflakes. A banana was sticking out of his ass.

Police suspect a cereal killer.

Bear Conference

Cambridge University was hosting a World's Bears Symposium. There were bear experts from all over the world. The Canadian Wildlife Service grizzly bear specialist, Art Pearson, had just given a paper on *The Grizzly Bears of Banff National Park, Alberta, Canada.*

During the coffee break after his delivery, Art was cornered by the Polish expert, Jan Polansky, and the Czechoslovakian expert, Miroslav Pospisil. These men wanted to know more about the high numbers of grizzlies in Banff compared to the low numbers in Europe.

These two secured permission from their governments to come to Canada to observe and do some behavioral studies on the Banff National Park grizzly bears. They flew to Calgary, took the bus to Banff and rented a room in a motel.

The next day, they started walking to the study area where Art Pearson had done his work. As they approached the area, a park warden stopped them to ask where they were going. They replied that they were going to study the grizzlies. The warden warned, "This is their mating season, so hold off for about a week." As they didn't budge, he suggested they walk back to Banff.

So, they started walking, and the warden took off in his truck. The moment he was out of sight, they turned around and headed back to the valley where the grizzlies are.

A day or so later, the manager of the motel reported to the Warden Service that the two Europeans are missing. One warden said, "Ohhhhh, no! I know where they went. Grab your rifles, guys, and come with me!" He led them to where he knew the two Europeans had gone.

Sure enough, within the first 100 metres there was a camera on the ground, then a pair of shoes, bits and pieces of clothing. The two bears were found just as they swallowed the last bits of the two men.

The bears were shot dead. Upon opening the female bear, the wardens found the remains of the Polish guy. One of the wardens then said, "That means the Czech is in the male."

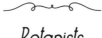

Botanists

A group of botanists had just returned from an expedition to the South Pacific Islands and was discussing their adventures with their colleagues back at the university where they taught.

"What was the most exciting discovery you found there?" asked a fellow professor.

One of them replied, "The people native to this one island had discovered the most amazing cure for constipation. Using only the leaves of the local palm trees, they concocted a suppository which quickly cured the ailment."

Another professor asked, "A palm leaf suppository? Did it really work?"

Replied the botanist, "With fronds like these . . . who needs enemas."

Book a Judge

An engaged couple went to a karaoke club. One of the attendees stood up and sang the greatest cover of "Stairway to Heaven" they had ever heard.

After the song, the couple asked the singer if he ever sang at weddings. Turns out he had recorded an album of his own love songs, and that he was a Justice of the Peace. So, he could marry them, too.

His songs were so bad that the couple's wedding was ruined. Their advice was never to book a judge by his cover.

Botanist Roy Noble

Botanist Roy Noble had always dreamt of ending world hunger. After years of research, his hard work paid off. He developed a strain of peas that would grow virtually any-where. It grew fast, kept long without spoiling, and was more nutritious than even soybeans. He was an instant hero, world-wide. There were awards and parades, and naturally the new strain of peas was named Noble.

After enjoying the fame and fortune for a while, Roy decided he wanted to do more, so he established a fund to award a monetary prize each year to botanists and hor-ticulturists who were making significant contributions to their fields.

Thus was born the famous Noble Peas Prize.

Breton Pikemen

When the Celtic, Breton-speaking pikemen returned to their ancestral lands and helped William the Conqueror win the Battle of Hastings, what were they carrying?

Answer: Brittany Spears

Bee & Wasp

"How are things going?" asked one bee of another.

"Terrible," replied the second bee. "I can't find any flowers or pollen or nectar anywhere."

"No problem," said the first bee. "Just fly down this street. There's a bar mitzvah going on with lots of flowers and fresh fruit."

"Thanks!" replied the second bee, buzzing off.

Later, the second bee thanked the first bee for the tip.

Then the first bee asked, "But what's that thing on your head?"

"My yarmulke," replied the second bee. "I didn't want them to think I was a wasp!"

Bumper Stickers You May Have Missed

If You Drink Don't Park. Accidents Cause People.

Impotence: Nature's Way Of Saying "No Hard Feelings."

The Earth Is Full - Go Home.

I Have The Body Of A God . Buddha.

The Face Is Familiar But I Can't Quite Remember My Name.

Illiterate? Write For Help.

I Refuse To Have A Battle Of Wits With An Unarmed Person.

You! Out of The Gene Pool!

I Do Whatever My Rice Krispies Tell Me To.

Where Are We Going And Why Am I In This Hand basket?

Remember Folks: Stop Lights Timed For 35mph Are Also Timed For 70mph and 140mph.

Necrophilia: That Uncontrollable Urge To Crack Open A Cold One.

Heart Attacks ... God's Revenge For Eating His Animal Friends.

Grow Your Own Dope. Plant a Man.

All Men Are Animals, Some Just Make Better Pets.

I used to have a handle on life, but it broke.

WANTED: Meaningful overnight relationship.

I need someone really bad...Are you really bad?

Beauty is in the eye of the beer holder.

Venison for dinner again? Oh, Deer!

England has no kidney bank, but it does have a Liverpool.

They told me I have Type A-blood, but it was a Typ-O.

I know a guy who's addicted to brake fluid, but he says he can stop anytime.

I stayed up all night to see where the sun went, then it dawned on me.

The girl said she recognized me from the vegetarian club, but I'd never met herbivore.

I'm reading a book about anti-gravity. It is so good I just can't put it down.

Velcro – what a rip off!

I went up a pole and came down a rushin'.

What do you call a dinosaur with an extensive vocabulary? A thesaurus.

The first job I ever had was working in an orange juice factory, but I was canned because I couldn't concentrate.

I then tried working in a muffler factory, but I found the work too exhausting.

I attempted work in a deli, but no matter which way I tried to slice it, I couldn't cut it.

After many years of trying to find steady work, I finally got job as a historian. The problem was that there was no future in it.

Tech Service Support

Tech Support: "I need you to right-click on the Open Desktop."

Customer: "OK."

Tech Support: "Did you get a pop-up menu?"

Customer: "No."

Tech Support: "OK. Right-click again. Do you now see a pop-up menu?"

Customer: "No."

Tech Support: "OK, sir. Can you tell me what you have done up to this point?"

Customer: "Sure, you told me to write 'click' and I wrote 'click.'"

Imperial and Metric Conversions

Ratio of an igloo's circumference to its diameter: Eskimo π.

1000 kg of Chinese soup: Won ton.

Time between slipping on a peel and smacking the pavement: 1 bananosecond.

Weight that an evangelist carries with God: 1 billigram.

362.25 days of drinking low-calorie beer: 1 lite year.

Half of a large intestine: 1 semicolon.

Basic unit of laryngitis: 1 hoarsepower.

1000 aches: 1 megahurtz.

1 million bicycles: 2 megacycles.

365.25 days: 1 unicycle.

10 cards: 1 decacards.

453.6 graham crackers: 1 pound cake.

2000 mockingbirds: 2 kilomockingbirds.

1 kg of falling figs: 1 Fig Newton.

1 millionth of a fish: 1 microfiche.

1 trillion pins: 1 terrapin.

100 rations: 1 C-ration.

2 monograms: 1 diagram.

8 nickels: 2 paradigms.

Time it takes to sail 220 yards at 1 nautical mile per hour: Knot-furlong.

2.4 statute miles of intravenous surgical tubing at Yale University Hospital: 1 I.V. League.

Butch the Rooster

John the farmer was in the fertilized-egg business. He had several hundred young layers (hens), called pullets, and 8 or 10 roosters, whose job it was to fertilize the eggs. The farmer kept records, and any rooster that didn't perform went into the soup and was replaced.

That took an awful lot of his time, so he bought a set of tiny bells and attached them to his roosters. Each bell had a different tone, so John could tell from a distance which rooster was performing. Now he could sit on the porch and fill out an efficiency report simply by listening to the bells.

The farmer's favorite rooster was Old Butch, and a very fine specimen he was, too. But on this particular morning, John noticed Old' Butch's bell hadn't rung at all! John went to investigate. The other roosters were chasing pullets, bells-a-ringing. The pullets, hearing the roosters coming, would run for cover. But to Farmer John's amazement, Butch had his bell in his beak, so it couldn't ring. He'd sneak up on a pullet, do his job, and walk on to the next one.

John was so proud of Old Butch, he entered him in the county fair, and Old Butch became an overnight sensation among the judges. The result...the judges not only awarded Old Butch the "No Bell Piece Prize." But they awarded him with the "Pulletsurprise" as well.

Clearly Old Butch was a politician in the making. Who else but a politician could figure out how to win two of the most highly coveted awards on our planet by being the best at sneaking up on the populace and screwing them while they weren't paying attention?

Folger's Coffee

A grandmother was surprised by her 7-year-old grandson one morning. He had made her coffee. She drank what was the worst cup of coffee in her life. When she got to the bottom, there were three of those little green army men in the cup.

She asked, "Honey, what are those army men doing in my coffee?" He replied, Grandma, it says on TV, 'The best part of waking up is the soldiers in your cup!' " (It's from an old commercial for "Folger's Coffee – Folgers in your Cup!")

Animal Crackers

When his Mum returned home with the groceries, the boy pulled out the box of animal crackers he had been begging for. He spread the animal-shaped crackers all over the kitchen counter.

"What are you doing?" his Mum asked.

He replied, "The box says you can't eat them if the seal is broken, so I'm looking for the seal."

The Holy Ghost

While walking along the sidewalk in front of his church, a Minister heard the intoning of a prayer that nearly made his collar wilt. Apparently his 5-year-old son and his play-mates had found a dead robin.

Feeling that proper burial should be performed, they had secured a small box and cotton batting, then dug a hole and made ready for the disposal of the deceased. The Minister's son was chosen to say the appropriate prayers and with sonorous dignity, intoned his version of what he thought his father always said:

"Glory be unto the Faaaather. And unto the Soooonnn . . . . . and into the hole he gooooooes."

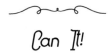

Can It!

A British food preservation expert came to Canada to see how we do things here. He started in the Maritimes in the many fish processing plants, worked his way west to Ontario to the huge southern Ontario food processing plants, saw the fast-freeze fresh water fish plants in Manitoba, then went on to BC.

In BC, he was taken to the huge salmon canneries in Prince Rupert. At the largest plant, at the end of the tour, the manager said, "We eat what we can, and what we can't, we can!" The Brit looked nonplussed said nothing.

On the way home in the plane, he exclaimed out loud as a look of considerable relief came over his face, "Oh! I get it!" Other passengers were wondering about him.

Back in his laboratory in the UK, the employees asked what he had learned in Canada. With puffed up pride, he said, "Funny people, those Canucks. They eat what they can, and what they can't, they tin!"

Change Streams

Two bacteria had been circling about very happily in the blood stream of a horse for some months. One asked the other if he had ever heard of the "lymph stream". The other replied that he had not.

They discussed it for a while, and decided to burrow over to try out the lymph stream. They travelled about half-way around the horse once and were killed by the lymph stream, proving that you should not change streams amid horse.

Chess Tournament

It was an international three-day chess tournament, and it was being held in the huge, open foyer of the Empire State Building in New York City. Many of the players knew one another from previous tournaments, so it was a social event as much as a tournament.

At the end of the first day's competition, many of the winners were sitting in the foyer, discussing, and yes, even bragging, about the winning moves they had made. After a few drinks, these normally quite and reserved players started becoming louder and louder - until the desk clerk could take no more. He then kicked them all out.

There were complaints from the players to the building management. They said that they had not been bothering anyone. The next morning the manager called the clerk in and mentioned the many complaints from the players. They said that the clerk had been rude, and that instead of kicking them out, he should have asked them to be less noisy.

The clerk replied, "I am sorry, sir, but if there is one thing I cannot stand, it's chess nuts boasting in an open foyer."

The Jacket

A young lady was a tour guide on a bus, which took her from Banff to Jasper and back three times per week. Her business attire was well-cut shorts and a jacket with the company logo on the front, along with her name. The bus stopped at Saskatchewan Crossing, and here the tourists could purchase meals and souvenirs. The stops at both ends were at cabins in the woods with a central camp-fire pit for sing fests and the like.

For the most part the tourists were retired and/or elderly, but on one occasion there were many younger tourists, some about her age. They invited her to come with them and they would buy her ice cream of her choice. She chose chocolate. As she left the ice cream store, she tripped, and got ice cream all over the front of her pretty jacket. She tried to rinse it out, but the chocolate color stood out on the light jacket.

That evening around the campfire, she got everyone's attention as took off her jacket and tossed it onto the fire. This caused a huge fire flare up. As soon as the fire died down a bit, one of the tourists said, "It was a blazer?"

The Religious Pet

A religious couple felt it was important to own an equally religious pet. So the visited a breeder and found a golden retriever they liked. When they asked the dog to fetch a Bible, he did it in a flash. When they instructed him to look up Psalm 23, he complied quickly, using his paws with dexterity. They were so impressed that they bought him.

That night they had friends over. They were so proud of their new dog and his skills that they showed him off a little. The friends were impressed and asked whether the dog was able to do any of the usual dog tricks as well. This stopped the couple cold, as they hadn't thought about normal tricks.

"Well," they said, "let's try this out." Once more they called the dog over and then clearly said the command, "Heel!"

Quick as a wink, the dog jumped up, put his paw on the man's forehead, closed his eyes in concentration and prayed.

How Many Wives?

A little boy was attending his first wedding. After the service, his cousin asked him, "How many women can a man marry?"

"Sixteen," the boy responded. His cousin was amazed that he had an answer so quickly. "How do you know that?"

"Easy," the little boy said. "All you have to do is add it up. It's like the Bishop said: 4 better; 4 worse; 4 richer; 4 poorer."

The Specialist

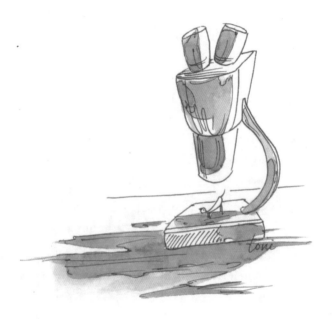

Q: What do you call someone who specializes in examining the rear ends of no-see-ums?

A: A Phlebotomist

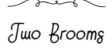

Two Brooms

Two brooms were hanging in a closet, and after a while, they came to know one another fairly well. They decided to get married.

One broom was the bride broom, and the other was the groom broom. The bride groom looked beautiful in her white dress, and the groom broom was very dapper in his tuxedo. The wedding was lovely.

After the wedding at the wedding dinner, the bride groom leaned over and said to the groom broom, "I think I am going to have a little whisk broom!"

"IMPOSSIBLE!" said the groom broom. "We haven't even swept together! It sounds to me like you have been sweeping around."

Christmas Stamps

A woman goes to the post office to buy stamps for her Christmas cards.

She says to the clerk, "May I have 50 Christmas stamps?"

The clerk says, "What denomination?"

The woman says, "God help us. Has it come to this??"

She then says, "Give me 6 Catholic, 12 Presbyterian, 10 Lutheran and 20 Baptists, and 2 Canadian"

Cinco de Mayo

Many stories have resulted from the tragic sinking of the great ship, the Titanic. Some are not as well-known as others. For example, most people don't know that back in 1912, Hellmann's Mayonnaise was manufactured in England. In fact, the Titanic was carrying 12,000 jars of the condiment scheduled for delivery in Vera Cruz, Mexico, which was to be the next port of call for the great ship after its stop in New York.

This shipment would have been the largest shipment ever exported to Mexico. The people of Mexico, who were crazy about the stuff, were eagerly awaiting delivery and were disconsolate at the loss; so much so, that they declared a National Day Of Mourning which they still observe today. It is known, of course, as Sinko de Mayo.

Claws and Clause

Biologists and grammarians have established a relation-ship between cats and grammar. They have found that with commas there is pause at the end of a clause, whereas with cats there are claws at the ends of the paws.

Elementary, Watson

Sherlock Holmes's sister, Ella, was a bit confused - not that she suffered from dementia or anything - she simply was a bit "blonde." She was always getting her two twins confused, even though they were fraternal, not identical, and everyone else could easily tell Patricia from Theresa.

One day Sherlock's sister invited the great detective and his assistant to a piano recital that Patsy was to give the following evening. When she left, Sherlock's assistant

said, rather bewilderedly, to Sherlock, "I didn't know Patsy was studying the piano." To which Holmes replied, "Ella meant Terry, my dear Watson."

Clydesdale Horse

A rancher bought a beautiful big, black Clydesdale horse, and brought her home. She had a very gentle personality. The first day he groomed her, washed her, and combed out her mane and tail till she looked like a million bucks.

When he came to see her the next morning, the horse was skittish, making it hard to approach her. He could hear birds tweeting and twittering in her stall. He saw that the birds had built nests in her mane. He was horrified. He led her out of the stall to where he had room to work on her. He combed out the nests, and groomed the horse again.

Next morning the birds were tweeting and twittering loudly, the nests were back, and the horse was twice as skittish as yesterday. He was at wits end, but he thought maybe his veterinarian friend could help, so he phoned him. The vet said, "Sprinkle yeast all over the mane every few days. The birds will leave and not come back."

So, after cleaning out the second batch of nests and birds and grooming the horse all over, he liberally sprinkled yeast all over the mane. Next morning there were no nests, and no birds. He was delighted.

A couple of weeks later, he ran into his vet friend in town, and asked him, "Say, just how does that yeast work to get rid of birds?" The vet replied, "It is simple! Yeast is yeast, and nest is nest, and never the mane shall tweet."

Computer Skills

Jesus and Satan were having an ongoing argument about who was better on the computer. They had been going at it for days, and God was tired of hearing all the bickering.

Finally, God said, "Cool it. I am going to set up a test which will take two hours, and I will judge who does the better job."

So Satan and Jesus sat down at the keyboards and typed away.

- They moused.
- They did spreadsheets.
- They wrote reports.
- They converted for export.
- They sent e-mail.
- They sent out e-mail with attachments.
- They downloaded.
- They browsed the TAXACOM archive.
- They made cards.
- They Googled.
- They did every known job.

But, ten minutes before the time was up, lightning suddenly flashed across the sky, thunder rolled, the rain poured, and, of course, the electricity went off.

Satan stared at his blank screen and screamed in every curse word known in the underworld.

Jesus just sighed.

The electricity finally flickered back on, and each of them restarted his computer.

Satan started searching frantically screaming, "It's gone! It's all gone! I lost everything when the power went out!"

Meanwhile, Jesus quietly started printing out all his files from the past two hours.

Satan observed this and became even more irate. "Wait! He cheated! How did he do it??!!"

God shrugged and said, "Jesus Saves."

Booth Paste

The driver of a huge tractor trailer lost control of his rig and plowed into an empty tollbooth, smashing it to pieces. Unhurt but a bit shaken up, he climbed down from the wreckage and looked around. Within a matter of minutes, another truck pulled up and unloaded a crew of workers. The men picked up each broken piece of the former tollbooth, spread some kind of creamy substance on it, and fitted the pieces together. In less than an hour, they had the entire tollbooth reconstructed and good as new.

"Astonishing!" said the truck driver to the crew chief.

"What was that white stuff you used to get all of the pieces together?"

The crew chief replied, "Tollgate booth paste."

Two Nuns in Europe

Two nuns, Sister Marilyn and Sister Helen, are travelling through Europe in a rented car. When they are in Transylvania and stopped at a traffic light, from out of nowhere a diminutive Dracula jumps up onto the hood of the car and hisses through the windscreen at them.

"Quick, quick!" shouts Sister Marilyn. "What'll we do?"

Sister Marilyn switches on the windscreen wipers, knocking Dracula about, but he clings on and continues to hiss at the nuns.

"What shall I do now?" shouts Sister Marilyn.

"Switch on the windscreen washer. I filled it with holy water in the Vatican," says Sister Helen.

Sister Marilyn turns on the windscreen washer. Dracula screams as the water burns his skin, but still he clings on and continues to hiss at the nuns.

"Now what?" shouts Sister Marilyn

"Show him your cross," says Sister Helen.

"Now you're talking," says Sister Marilyn as she opens the window and screams loudly,

"Get the hell off our car!"

Ground Hog Day

A certain Milwaukee delicatessen served beef burgers. On February 2, 1886, they ran out of beef. The manager found a ham, put it through the grinder, and served it between buns. When customers asked what the sandwich

was called, she replied "hamburgers." The deli went back to beef, but since that day, February 2 has always been celebrated as ground hog day.

Hare Today

A man is driving along a highway and sees a rabbit jump out across the middle of the road. He swerves to avoid hitting it, but unfortunately the rabbit jumps right in front of the car. The driver, a sensitive man as well as an animal lover, pulls over to find out what has become of the rabbit. Much to his sorrow, the rabbit is dead.

The driver feels so awful that he begins to cry. A beautiful blonde woman driving down the highway sees a man crying on the side of the road and pulls over. She steps out of the car and asks the man what's wrong.

"I feel terrible," he explains, "I accidentally hit this rabbit and killed it."

The blonde says, "Don't worry." She runs to her car and pulls out a spray can. She walks over to the limp, dead rabbit, bends down and sprays the contents onto the rabbit.

The rabbit jumps up, waves its paw at the two of them and hops off down the road. Three metres away the rabbit stops, turns around and waves again. He hops down the road another 3 metres, turns and waves, hops another 3 metres, turns and waves, and repeats this again and again and again, until he finally hops off out of sight.

The man is astonished. He runs over to the woman and demands, "What is in that can? What did you spray on that rabbit?"

The woman turns the can around so that the man can read the label.

It says:

"Hair Spray - Restores life to dead hair, and adds a permanent wave."

He Makes the Coffee

When they awoke on the first day of married life, she said, "Well, hon, it is your job to make the coffee. It says so in the Bible."

"Where does it say that?" he demanded to know.

"Hebrews," she replied.

He Tunes But Once

A lady was planning a huge afternoon and evening party. Much of the work had been handed out to caterers. On the morning of the event, she sat down at her piano to relax and play a few tunes. There was to be a professional piano player playing at the event.

After playing a few notes, she discovered to her horror that the piano had several notes out of tune. She phoned several piano tuners, only to find that all were booked. Finally she connected with a man, the owner of Oppornockerty Piano Tuning, who could come out right away.

He arrived, and in short order had the piano in perfect order. He played a tune for her, and then had her play for herself, just to confirm. All was well. She even gave him a large tip over and above the billing for being so prompt and doing such a wonderful tuning.

About an hour before the party, she again sat the piano and played, only to discover that different notes were now no longer in tune. She phoned Mr Oppornockerty, and pleaded with him to come and retune the piano.

Despite her pleas, he declined, saying, "Oppornockerty tunes but once."

Henry Ford

Other than Swiss-born Louis Chevrolet, Henry Ford was one of only a very few people in the world who could say that he wrote an autobiography.

Moses and George W

George W. Bush was walking through an airport, when he saw an old man with long white hair, a long white beard, was wearing a long, white robe and was holding a staff. Bush walked up to the old man, who was staring at the ceiling, and asked, "Excuse me, sir, aren't you Moses?"

The old man continued to stare at the ceiling, saying nothing. Again George W asked, a little louder, "Excuse me, sir, aren't you Moses?" The old man continued to stare at the ceiling, motionless, and without saying a word.

George W tried a third time, louder yet. "Excuse me, sir, aren't you Moses?" No movement or words came from the old man. He continued to stare at the ceiling. One of George W's aides asked him if there is a problem, and George W said, "Either this man is deaf or extremely rude. I've asked him three times if he was Moses, and he hasn't answered me yet."

To which the man, still staring at the ceiling finally replied, "I can hear you, and yes, I am Moses, but the last time I spoke to a bush, I spent 40 years wandering in the wilderness."

Copying

A new monk arrives at the monastery. He is assigned to help the other monks in copying the old texts by hand. He notices, however, that they are copying copies, and not the original books. So, the new monk goes to the head monk to ask him about this.

He points out that if there was an error in the first copy, that error would be continued in all of the other copies. The head monk says, "We have been copying from the copies for centuries, but you make a good point, my son."

The next day the head monk goes down into the cellar with one of the copies to check it against the original.

Hours later, nobody has seen him. One of the other monks goes downstairs to look for him and hears a sobbing coming from the back of the cellar. He finds the old monk leaning over one of the original books crying.

"How am I going to tell them the word is **CelebRate**"

Home Surgery Book

The federal and provincial governments have been exploring ways to cut back on the high costs of medicare. To this end, they have gotten together to publish a well-illustrated little book that gives surgery instructions that can be done at home.

The book costs $6, and is titled, "Suture Self".

Howls of Protest

"Wolf sterilization experiment dropped after howls of protest," article headline, The Edmonton Journal, 25 October 2009, page B9. Origin: Cathy Ellis, Calgary Herald. Banff.

Stealing Art

Did you hear about the guy who almost got away with stealing several paintings from the Louvre? After planning the crime, and getting in and out past security, he was captured just two blocks away when his van ran out of gas.

Asked how he could mastermind such a crime and then make such an obvious error, he replied:

"Monsieur, I had no Monet to buy Degas to make the Van Gogh."

And you thought I lacked De Gaulle to tell a story like that?

I de Falla to un-Ravel that mess.

Deas Island Tunnel

In the late 1950s, concrete sections were made, taken to the site, and then sunk into a channel that had been dug in the riverbed the Fraser River Delta in BC. After the sections were connected and drained, they became what is known as the Deas Island Tunnel. It is an under-river, or river-bottom tunnel.

Being so low (actually, below sea level) caused some problems with removing exhaust fumes from so many vehicles. Soon it became obvious that a specialist in exhaust filtering in tunnels was needed to solve the problem. The exhaust specialist connected all the testing equipment where large exhaust out-take tubes were supposed to suck out all the exhaust fumes from the tunnel. His main purpose was to see just what the exhaust out-takes were removing, and more importantly, what they were not removing, from the tunnel.

There was trouble with one of the sets of testing equipment, so he climbed the ladder to see if he could fix it. When he reached over to touch the on-off switch, he slipped and fell to the concrete below, killing him instantly.

He was such a noted specialist that his death was announced very widely and quickly. Before he could be taken to the undertaker, a noted brain surgeon at McGill University called to ask if he could examine the brain of this exhaust and filtering expert. He said this would give him a rare and wonderful opportunity to examine the brain of a filtering man's thinker.

Indian Artifacts

Artifacts are a major portion of an Indian reservation's economy. Annually, thousands of tourists visit reservations, and most will not leave without purchasing at least one memento of the traditional Indian culture.

One enterprising Indian was able to outsell his competitors in the sale of wooden dolls by selling them at only a fraction of the cost others had to charge. On examination of his dolls they found that where traditionally hard wood was used, this Indian would use cheap pine on which he glued thin pieces of fine oak, thus being able to produce the dolls at only a fraction of the cost.

While he claimed his dolls were still authentic, his competitors complained that they were only a cheap Sioux Veneer.

Indy 500

A young Native American woman went to a doctor for her first ever physical exam. After checking all of her vitals and running the usual tests, the doctor said, "Well, Running Doe, you are in fine health. I could find no problems. I did notice one abnormality, however."

"Oh, what is that, Doctor?"

"Well, you have no nipples."

"None of the people in my tribe has ..... nipples," she replied.

"That is amazing," said the doctor. "I'd like to write this up for The South Dakota Journal of Medicine if you don't mind." She said, "OK."

"First of all," asked the doctor, "how many people are in your tribe?"

She answered, "Approximately 500."

"And what is the name of your tribe?" asked the doctor.

Running Doe replied, "We're called *The Indiannippleless Five Hundred*."

Interesting Punny Signs

On a septic tank truck: Yesterday's Meals on Wheels.

On a plumber's truck: We repair what your husband fixed.

On another plumber's truck: Don't sleep with a drip. Call me.

On a church bill board: 7 days without God makes one weak.

On an electrician's truck: Let us remove your shorts.

On a fence: Salesmen welcome! Dog food is expensive.

At an optometrist's office: If you can't see what you are looking for, you're at the right place.

At a car dealership: The best way to get back on your feet - miss a car payment.

At a radiator shop: Best place in town to take a leak.

On the back of another septic tank truck: Caution - This Truck is full of Political Promises.

Did you hear about the cellist who used cat gut to string his cello rather than metal? His motto is: In gut we trust.

The End is Near

A local priest and a pastor were fishing on the side of the road. They thoughtfully made a sign saying, "The End is Near. Turn yourself around now before it's too late!"

One driver who drove by didn't appreciate the sign and shouted at them as he drove past, "Leave us alone, you religious nuts!"

All of a sudden they heard a big SPLASH! The priest and the pastor looked at each other, and one asked, "Do you think we should just put up a sign that says, 'Bridge Out' instead?"

Patient Patient

A man rushed to his doctor's office, and said to the receptionist, "I gotta see Dr Jones really soon. I think I am shrinking!"

The receptionist replied, "Keep calm, Mr Smith. There are a couple of people before you. You have to be a little patient today."

Penguins

Did you ever wonder why there you never see dead penguins on the ice in pictures from Antarctica? Wonder no more.

It is a known fact that penguins lead a very ritualistic life that is extremely ordered and complex. Penguins are very committed to their families, will mate for life, and will form and maintain a form of compassionate contact with their offspring.

If a penguin is found dead on the ice surface, other members of the family and immediate social circle will dig holes in the ice by using their beaks and vestigial wings. When the hole is deep enough, the dead bird is rolled up to the edge of the hole.

The male penguins then gather in a circle around the fresh grave and sing:

"Freeze a jolly good fellow.
Freeze a jolly good fellow."

Then they kick him in the ice hole and bury him.

Iraq Civil War

In Iraq, as long as the Shias and Sunnis are embroiled in a civil war, the Kurds will have their own whey.

Psalm 23

Timmy was a little five year old boy that his Mom loved very much. Being an obsessive worrier, his mother was quite concerned about him walking to school when he first started kindergarten.

She walked him to school the first couple of days, but when he came home the second day, he told his mother that he did not want her walking him to school every day. He wanted to be like the "big boys." He protested loudly, so she thought of an idea of how to handle it.

She asked a neighbor, Mrs Goodnest, if she would surreptitiously follow her son to school, at a distance behind him that he would not likely notice, but close enough to keep a watch on him. Mrs Goodnest thought that since she was up early with her toddler anyway, it would be a good way for them to get some exercise as well, so she agreed.

The next school day, Mrs Goodnest and her little girl, Marcy, set out following behind Timmy as he walked to school with another neighbor boy he knew. She did this for the rest of the week.

On Friday, as the boys walked and chatted, kicking stones and twigs, the little friend of Timmy again noticed that the lady and little girl were following them, just as they had been doing for the last three days.

Finally, he said to Timmy, "Have you noticed that lady and little girl following us the last few days? Do you know them?"

Timmy nonchalantly replied, "Yeah, I know who they are."

The little friend said, "Well who are they then?"

"That's just Shirley Goodnest and her daughter, Marcy," replied Timmy.

The little friend asked, "Marcy, and her mother, Shirley Goodnest? Who in the heck are they, and why are they following us to kindergarten each day?"

"Well," Timmy explained, "every night my Mom makes me say the 23rd Psalm with my prayers because she worries about me so much. And in the Psalm, it says, "Shirley Goodnest and Marcy shall follow me all the days of my life. So I guess I'll just have to get used to it."

It Could Happen

A neutron walked into a bar and ordered a beer.

"How much?" asked the neutron.

"No charge!" replied the barkeep.

I've Found Cod

Far away in the tropical waters of the Caribbean, two prawns were swimming around in the sea, one called Justin and the other called Christian. The prawns were constantly being harassed and threatened by sharks that inhabited the area.

Finally, one day Justin said to Christian, "I'm fed up with being a prawn, I wish I were a shark, and then I wouldn't have any worries about being eaten." A large, mysterious cod appeared and said, "Your wish is granted"

And Lo! And behold! Justin turned into a shark. Horrified, Christian immediately swam away, afraid of being eaten by his old mate. Time passed (as it invariably does) and Justin found life as a shark boring and lonely. All his old mates simply swam away whenever he came close to them. Justin didn't realize that his new menacing appearance was the cause of his sad plight.

While swimming alone one day, he saw the mysterious cod again, and he thought perhaps the mysterious fish could change him back into a prawn. He approached the cod and begged to be changed back. And Lo and Behold, he found himself turned back into a prawn. With tears of joy in his tiny little eyes Justin swam back to his friends and bought them all a cocktail. Looking around the gathering at the reef, he realized he couldn't see his old pal.

"Where's Christian?" he asked. "He's at home, still distraught that his best friend changed sides to the enemy and became a shark," they replied. Eager to put things right again and end the mutual pain and torture, he set off to Christian's house. As he opened the coral gate, the memories came flooding back.

He banged on the door and shouted, "Justin. It's me! Your old friend! Come out and see me again."

Christian replied, "No way man, you'll eat me. You're a shark, and therefore the enemy. I'll not be tricked into being your dinner."

Justin cried back, "No, I'm not. That was the old me. I've changed............I've found Cod. I'm a Prawn again Christian".

King Ozymandias

King Ozymandias of Assyria was running low on cash after years of war with the Hittites. His last great possession was the Star of the Euphrates, the most valuable diamond in the ancient world.

Desperate, he went to Crosus, the pawn-broker, to ask for a loan.

Crosus said, "I'll give you 100,000 dinars for it!"

"But I paid a million dinars for it," the King protested.

"Don't you know who I am? I am the King!"

Crosus replied, "When you wish to pawn a Star, makes no difference who you are."

Las Vegas Churches

This may come as a surprise to those of you not living in Las Vegas, but there are more Catholic churches than there are casinos.

Not surprisingly, some worshippers at Sunday services will give casino chips rather than cash when the basket is passed. Since these churches get chips from many different casinos, the churches have devised a method to collect the offerings.

The churches send all their collected chips to a nearby Franciscan Monastery for sorting, and then the chips are taken to the casinos of origin and cashed in. This is done by the chip monks.

Cowboy Joe

Israeli police are looking for a man named Joseph, wanted for looting in the port city of Haifa. The suspect is described as the son of an ex-nun from Barcelona and a German father. He was a former flutist and worked occasionally as a cowboy. In short, he was a Haifa-lootin, flutin Teuton, son of a nun from Barcelona, part time cowboy Joe. (GRN)

Layman Talk

The minister said to his wife, "I'm to give a talk to a room full of layman church members this evening, but I cannot find my clerical collar."

His wife replied, "Oh, no! You will be a lay date and a collar short!"

109

Legal Problems

An attorney was driving through the country side when his car failed him. He looked under the hood and knocked a few items around with a hammer. In the process he knocked off a gas line and got his arm soaked with gas before getting it back on. Discouraged, he attempted to start his car.

Much to his surprise, it started and he headed for the nearest town for a permanent repair. To celebrate his success, he lit up a cigarette, at which time his arm exploded into flames. He stuck his arm out the window hoping the wind at 80 km per hour would put it out.

He was promptly pulled over by a local constable and given a ticket for an illegal use of a firearm.

Lice on Leaf

Henry was an entomologist at the local university. He was to be up for promotion this year and with the promotion would come tenure. But there was a problem.

It was not that he could not teach – indeed, two years ago he had been honored by the undergraduates by being named their favorite teacher. No, his problem was with his research. He had not had a successful research project in several years, and in this day of "Publish or Perish" this was not a good situation. So that day, feeling depressed, he left the university as soon as his morning lecture was over, so that he could work in his garden. This always had been effective at relieving tension in the past. But to his

chagrin, he found most of his roses were dying, and on further examination found they were infested.

But what were these insects? They appeared to belong to the Suborder Anoplura, the sucking lice. That was strange, as Anoplura feed on animals, not plants.

He re-examined them more closely. Small, wingless, definitely a species of *Pediculus*, but one he had never seen before. He gathered up several specimens, and rushed to his lab, full of new vigor. He examined them in detail and rapidly wrote an article describing this new species. Well, I'm sure you know the result. The article was immediately accepted by the journal. His job was saved, and he received his most coveted tenure. And he received a new major grant to study this new species.

You could say he had discovered a new lice on leaf.

Swine Flu

There is a lot of misinformation being sent to people regarding swine flu - what to do and what not to do, what is safe to eat and what is not safe to eat.

The Health Department advises that you may receive an email purportedly from them (the Health Department) advising not to eat canned pork. The Health Department has not sent out any such message, so ignore it – it's just spam.

Serious Burns Unit

An English doctor is being shown around a Scottish hospital. He goes to examine the first patient he sees, and the man proclaims:

"Fair fa' yer sonsie face,
Great chieftain e' the puddin' race!"

The Englishman, somewhat taken aback, goes to the next patient, who immediately launches into:

"Some hae meat, and canna eat,
And some wad eat that want it,
But we hae meat and we can eat,
And sae the Lord be thankit."

The next patient sits up and declaims:

"Wee sleekit cow'rin tim'rous beastie,
O what a panic's in thy breastie!
Thou need na start awa sae hasty,
wi' bickering brattle.
I wad be laith to run and chase thee,
wi'murdering prattle!"

The Englishman says to his Scottish colleague, "I take it this is the psychiatric ward?"

"Ooooooooh Noooooo," the Scotsman corrects him, "it's the Serious Burns Unit."

Tacoma YMCAs

A Tacoma, WA, father was very proud to see his daughter graduate high school, but disturbed that she wanted to attend a fancy college in MA. Hoping to convince her to stay at home (and avoiding the astronomical tuition at the eastern school), he offered her membership in both Tacoma branches of the YMCA. She loves unlimited workouts well enough to accept the latter. That proves that she loved ….. not Wellesley but Two Y's. (GRN)

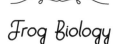

Frog Biology

A noted biologist, who had been studying little green frogs in a swamp, was stumped. The frog population, despite efforts at predator control, was declining at an alarming rate.

A chemist at a nearby college came up with a solution: The frogs, because of a chemical change in the swamp water, simply couldn't stay coupled long enough to reproduce successfully.

The chemist then brewed up a new adhesive to assist the frogs' togetherness, which included one part sodium. It seems the little green frogs needed some monosodium glue to mate.

Nagivator

A woman, who does not drive, is a noted backseat driver. She tells you how fast to drive, when to turn, road conditions, the works, never-endingly. On one memorable occasion, she was on a trip with her daughter, and her son-in-law was driving. He had dutifully held his tongue.

When asked by the man's sister if they had had any trouble along the trip, the son-in-law said, "Oh, no. I had help from the nagivator."

Pearly Gate Paste

When George died, he proceeded straight to the pearly gates, where he was met by St. Peter.

St Peter welcomed George, and then made a surprising revelation: Those famous pearly gates are, in fact, not free and open to the public. To get past them you have to pay a fee.

"Of course, it's a small matter," said St Peter, "and everyone who comes through is able to pay. But I have a deal for you. It's the same deal I offer everyone, but no one's been able to take me up on it yet."

He led George over to a tollbooth, and there, where the gate adjoined the booth, was a huge crack in the wall of the booth. The gate itself, similar to the swinging arm of the railroad crossing, was stuck and was sagging in a bent-down position.

"The gate hasn't operated properly for centuries because of this," said St Peter. "I tell anyone who comes through that he can come in free if he can fix it for me. So far no one's been able to do it."

George, always well prepared, had brought a bag with him, and he reached into it and brought out a tube, from which he extracted a creamy, gooey substance. He worked the substance liberally into the crack where the gate adjoined the booth, and, *mirabile dictu*, in mere moments St Peter was able to raise and lower the gate freely. It was good as new.

"Astonishing!" said St Peter. "You get to enter free of charge. But tell me. What was that white stuff you used to fix it?"

George smiled, and said, "That stuff? Oh, it's just a little Pearly Gate Booth Paste."

And he went inside. (RCC)

Tate's Compass

Back in the early 1840s, the Tate Watch Company of New York made a good pocket watch in a nickel-steel case that kept really good time. The watch could be sat on, or suffer other indignities, yet would not be damaged and would still keep good time. And because of the durability of the case, engravings did not wear thin, as they did with softer metals. Tate watches were handed down over the years to family members, retaining all the original qualities.

Because so many people were heading west in the U.S.A. in the late 1840s, the Tate Watch Company decided to include a small compass in the watch case. The Company did not realize that the nickel-steel case would affect the magnetic aspects of the compass, and neither did those who purchased a Tate watch and compass.

Using the Tate watch and compass on their way west, the owners could always tell what time it was, but many became lost, winding up in the Prairies of Canada, or the banks of the Rio Grande River. Thus the origin of the expression, *He who has a Tate's is lost.*

NASA Planning

Did you hear that NASA is planning to send a herd of Holsteins into orbit? Apparently they are calling it the herd shot 'round the world.

Newspaper Headline

Tired of being broke and stuck in an unhappy marriage, a young man named Henry decided to solve both problems by taking out a large insurance policy on his wife, with himself as the beneficiary, then arranging to have her killed.

A "friend of a friend" put him in touch with the nefarious "Artie," who explained that his price is $5,000. Henry said he would gladly pay Artie that, but he wouldn't have any cash until he collected on his wife's insurance policy. Artie insisted on being paid at least something up front, so when Henry opened his wallet, there was but a single loonie! Artie sighed, rolled his eyes, then said that this committed Henry to paying the rest. Henry agreed.

Artie started following Henry's wife around to get an idea of her habits, and after three days, decided to do the deed in the supermart. He surprised her in the produce section, strangling her with his gloved hands. The manager of the produce section stumbled onto the scene, and Artie, unwilling to leave a witness, murdered him, too.

Unknown to Artie, the entire action was captured on hidden security cameras, and was watched by the store's security guard, who immediately called police. Artie was caught and arrested even before he left the store.

Under questioning at the police station, Artie revealed the whole, sordid plan, including his rather unusual financial arrangements with Henry, who was also quickly arrested.

The next day, the newspaper headline read, "ARTIE CHOKES 2 FOR $1 AT SUPERMART".

Oliver Twist

Charles Dickens has this great idea for a novel, but can't come up with the right name for his lead character. No matter how he tries, no name seems just right. In despair, he leaves his apartment and strolls to the neighborhood pub, where he orders a martini. The bartender asks him a question, and he dashes out, back to his apartment, and begins writing his novel.

What did the bartender ask him?

Answer: "Olive or twist?" (GRN)

Counting Sheep

A sheep farmer started wondering how many sheep he has in his field, so he asked the sheepdog to count them.

The dog ran into the field, counted them, and then ran back to his master.

"So," asked the farmer, "how many sheep are there?"

121

"40," replied the dog.

"What? How can there be 40?" exclaimed the farmer. "I bought only 38!"

"I know," replied the dog, "but I rounded them up."

No Peace for the Wicked

It's Harvest Sunday at a small village church in rural England, and the vicar is organizing his annual harvest service, where people bring their home-grown plants and vegetables to the service.

But this year is different. The local village cricket team has just won their league, and the village is in celebratory mood, so the vicar decides to do something special - he will combine the normal harvest service with a cricket theme.

The day of the service arrives, and the church is filled with flowers. People are bringing in their offerings of vegetables, and in the middle of the display is a cricket wicket; a strip of turf with a set of wooden stumps at each end, and people are laying their offerings on the wicket.

Everything is going fine until one lady comes up to the front of the church and places a bag of frozen peas among the other vegetables. She is stopped by the vicar, so she returns to her seat, still clutching her peas.

"What happened?" asked the lady she's sitting next to.

She shrugs her shoulders, and says, "There's no peas for the wicket."

Noah and the New Ark

One day God calls down to Noah and says, "Noah, me old china, I want you to make me a new Ark."

Noah replies, "No probs, God, me old Supreme Being; anything you want. After all, you're the guv'...."

But God interrupts, "Ah, but there's a catch. This time, Noah, I want not just a couple of decks, I want 20 decks one on top of the other".

"20 DECKS!", screams Noah. "Well, OK, Big Man, whatever you say. Should I fill it up with all the animals just like last time?"

"Yep, that's right, well . . . sort of right . . . this time I want you to fill it up with fish," God answers.

"Fish?", queries Noah

"Yep, fish ... well, to make it more specific, Noah. I want Carp - wall to wall, floor to ceiling -Carp!"

Noah looks to the skies. "OK, God, my old mucker, let me get this right, you want a New Ark?"

"Check."

"With 20 decks, one on top of the other?"

"Check."

"And you want it full of Carp?"

"Check."

"Why?" asks the perplexed Noah, who was slowly but surely getting to the end of his tether.

"Dunno," says God. "I just fancied a Multi-Storey Carp Ark."

New Toyota

Why the new Toyota hybrid (gas/electric) is not made in the U.S.A.?

Because if it were, it would be a *nisei prius*. (GRN)

Jack Jax

Dr Tom Smith is a biologist, and his specialty is classification of lady-bird beetles. He works in a small college, and about once per month or so he produces a paper describing one or more new species of lady-bird beetles. Sometimes he describes a new genus.

Each time a new paper comes out in which at least one new taxon is described, he tacks up a copy on the departmental bulletin board for all to see and enjoy. The plates in these taxonomic papers are in color, beautifully showing the pretty lady-bird beetles.

As his tacked up taxonomic papers are taking a lot of room on the one and only bulletin board, the department head decides to put up a second bulletin board that faces the first. In short order Smith, who had filled up all the space on the first bulletin board, starts tacking up his papers on the new board.

The head of the department is furious and frustrated at this abuse of space, so he decides to charge Smith $20 for each tacked-up paper. When Smith complains, he is told that it is a taxon tax on tacks.

Subsequent graffiti, written by Smith, but blamed on students, read,

"Down with attacks on taxon tax on tacks."

Roy Rogers

"More hay, Trigger?"

"No thanks, Roy, I'm stuffed!"

Old Habits

Several elderly nuns were in their second floor convent one night when a fire broke out. They took their habits off, tied them together to make a rope, and climbed out the window.

After they were safely on the ground and out of the building, a news reporter came over to one of the nuns and said to her, "Weren't you afraid that the habits could have ripped or torn since they are old?

The nun replied, "Nah, don't you know old habits are hard to break?"

Legal Concerns

The Bureau of Alcohol, Tobacco, and Firearms (BATF) seized an extraordinary number of illegal firearms, consisting of Colts, Glocks, Taurus and Winchesters -- but they successfully prosecuted only the owners of the pistols. Cases against the owners of the Winchesters were all dismissed. Why?

Answer: The law does not concern itself with rifles. (RCC)

Excited Reception

Two aerial antennas met on a roof, fell in love and got married. The ceremony wasn't much, but the reception was excellent.

Jumper Cable

A jumper cable walks into a bar. The bartender says "I'll serve you, but don't start anything."

Food Not Served Here

A sandwich walks into a bar. The bartender says, "Sorry, we don't serve food in here."

One for the Road

A man walks into a bar with a slab of asphalt under his arm and says: "A beer please, and one for the road."

Funny-Tasting Food

Two cannibals are eating a clown. One says to the other: "Does this taste funny to you?"

Nothing to Look At

An invisible man marries an invisible woman. The kids are nothing to look at either.

Cross-Eyed Dog

A man takes his Rottweiler to the vet and says, "My dog's cross- eyed, is there anything you can do for him?" "Well," says the vet, "let's have a look at him." So he picks the dog up and examines his eyes, then checks his teeth. Finally, he says "I'm going to have to put him down." "What? Because he's cross-eyed?"

"No, because he's really heavy."

Hard-to-Find Pants

I went to buy some camouflage trousers the other day but I couldn't find any.

Skinny Plants

Q: Why aren't plants fat?

A: Because they are light eaters.

Perfection

Don't worry about being Nobody. Nobody is perfect.

Seafood Buffet

I went to a seafood buffet at the gymnasium last week............and pulled a mussel.

Bar Food

Two termites walk into a bar. One asked, "Is the bar tender here?"

Predatory Lion

It seems that a tribe in East Africa had trouble with a predatory lion attacking their livestock. It would kill and eat a cow and then show off its masculinity by coupling with various lionesses of his pride. The villagers tried to use one another as bait, in hopes of being able to kill the beast, but Mr. Lion was having none of it. They heard that the Queen was on a tour of the country and audaciously kidnapped her (the Palace put a news blackout on the matter). But tying her to a tree failed to entice the maned creature. This proves that:

Some people can't draw a straight lion with a ruler. (GRN)

The Son 'll Come Out

The star of the old TV series *Combat* was on the set when he got an urgent call from home. It seems that his little boy had locked himself in the closet and couldn't be persuaded to unlock the door. Everything else had been tried; finally they had to resort to calling Dad home from work. Why?

Answer: Because the son'll come out to Morrow. GRN)

Tomorrow in Mindanao

Fearing another uprising by a tribe on the Island of Mindanao, the Philippine Government today sent 50 armed troops to suppress the uprising. The battle lasted for less than two days. The first day, 42 Government troops were captured, and the other 8 will be captured by two Moro.

Political Cognoscenti

The tiny Massachusetts village of Bone has long been known by the political cognoscenti as the only municipality that has voted for the winner in each Presidential election since 1791, including the election of 2002. Does Mitt Romney's Bay State defeat of Shannon O'Brien support the idea that women are more likely than men to lose Bone, Mass? (GRN)

Way to Go, Kate

Kate Middleton of the British Royal Family, also known as the Duchess of Cambridge, declared about a week or so before the birth of her second child that she had just made her last official public appearance. It was called a Pregnant Pause.

Slow-Moving Cyclists

Cyclists who moved slowly uphill on the Banff-Jasper Highway in Canada's Mountain National Parks do so at their own risk as they are in grizzly bear country. This gives a whole new meaning to the phrase "Meals on Wheels".

Enterprise Crew Evaluation

When I saw the crew of Enterprise meet the Borg, I though back to the Voyager episodes in which Jeri Ryan played the Borg who became human. She was obviously on the show only for her sex appeal. Most people called her a ten. Personally, I thought she had a flaw in her beauty and rated her only a nine. But her unsmiling nature reminded me of a certain famous actor.

She was an earnest Borg Nine. (GRN)

Militant Girl Dancers

What does it take to do the advanced math needed to calculate exactly how many militant Jewish girls should dance in the Radio City Music Hall chorus line?

A Rockette Zionist. (RCC)

Attorney Rehab Clinic

What does a drug and alcohol recovery clinic catering solely to lawyers have that's like a well-known birthday greeting?

Many attorney rehabs. (RCC)

A New University Medical Department

The University announced today the creation of a new department in the Faculty of Medicine. It will be called The Department of Tetrapyloctomy. The University created the new department as part of he reaction to provincial and federal governments' continuing financial cuts to medical faculties and to medicare. The function of the new department is to inculcate a sense of irreverence in graduate tetrapyloctomy students. In turn, they will develop useless medical techniques. If you can't win arguments by splitting proverbial hairs, employ a tetrapyloctomist.

Boating Accident

As you are probably aware, I have been sailing/racing boats all my life.

I have seen a lot of great things happen on the water, but I will never forget the boating accident between the yacht, Red Dawn, and the schooner, Blue Lagoon. It left the survivors marooned.

Cold Turkey

A teenager with a reputation for having a bottomless pit when eating food was asked by his mum if he wanted some of the turkey leftovers from Thanksgiving.

He replied, "Thanks, but no thanks. Last night I ate 1 drumstick, 2 thighs, 2 wings and a plateful of white meat. "

So his mum asked if he wanted something else, and he replied, "Yes, please. I am quitting cold turkey."

Convoluted Art

A high-end art store, The Art Palace, sells art on themes of zoology and astronomy in one work. On Saturdays, The Art Palace has a promotion: if a customer can guess what today's colors are, he or she will receive a gift of two men's hairpieces.

A customer, who had phoned in an order, arrives in the afternoon and says, "I am here to pick up the two prints of whales and suns! Are the toupé rinses black?"

The startled clerk asks, "Black? How could they possibly be black?

The customer replies, "Because of dye!"

The clerk says, "But their mother wasn't black. Anyway, you have come to the wrong palace. They are not here. Go to the big square building in London."

Contractions

His wife was in labor with their first child. Things were going pretty well when she suddenly she began to shout:

"Shouldn't"

"Couldn't"

"Wouldn't"

"CAN'T"

"Doctor, what's wrong with my wife?" asked the disturbed father-to-be.

"It's perfectly normal," the doctor reassured him. "She's just going through her contractions."

Bulls: Pampus, Pompous

What is the difference between the speeches of Howard Dean and the nickname of the one-time Argentinean boxer Luis Firpo?

There is very little difference. One is the Wild Bull of the Pampas; the other, the wild bull of the pompous. (GRN)

Two Catholic Boys

There were two Catholic boys, Timothy Murphy and Antonio Secola, whose lives parallel each other in amazing ways. In the same year Timothy was born in Ireland, Antonio was born in Italy. Faithfully they attended parochial school from kindergarten through their senior year in high school.

They took their vows to enter the priesthood early in college, and upon graduation, became priests.

Their careers had come to amaze the world, but it was generally acknowledged that Antonio Secola was just a cut above Timothy Murphy in all respects. Their rise through the ranks of Bishop, Archbishop, and finally Cardinal, was swift to say the least, and the Catholic world knew that when the present Pope died, it would be one of the two who would become the Next Pope.

In time the Pope did die, and the College of Cardinals went to work. In less time than anyone had expected, white smoke rose from the Chimney, and the world waited to see whom they had chosen.

The world, Catholic, Protestant and secular, was surprised to learn that Timothy Murphy had been elected Pope!

Antonio Secola was beyond surprise. He was devastated, because even with all of Timothy's gifts, Antonio knew he was the better qualified. With gall that shocked the Cardinals, Antonio Secola asked for a private session with them in which he candidly asked, "Why Timothy?"

After a long silence, an old Cardinal took pity on the bewildered man and rose to reply. "We knew you were the better of the two, but we just could not bear the thought of the leader of the Roman Catholic Church being called Pope Secola."

Viking Explorer

A famous Viking explorer, Leif, sails home, after years spent on an adventurous voyage, to find that his name is unaccountably missing from his town's register. His wife insists that he complain to the local civic official.

The official apologizes profusely, saying,

"I must have taken Leif off my census."

William Tell

Historical records show that William Tell and his family were all avid bowlers. Unfortunately, all the league records were destroyed in a fire. Now we will never know for whom the Tells bowled.

No Negotiating with Terriers

At the local humane society, a giant schnauzer has locked an attendant in a cage and is holding him hostage, while keeping other attendants at bay and demanding better food and a suitable adoption placement.

Why does the society ignore these demands?

They refuse to negotiate with terriers.

Escargot

A snail went into a Volkswagen dealership to look at the new Rabbit models. He found one he liked, and called the salesman over and said, "I want this Rabbit model, and I am willing to pay cash. But, I want you to take all the rabbit icons off, all of the letter R's, and have them replaced with a snail icon, and the letter S."

"I am afraid that cannot be done, sir,"

The snail replied, "I am willing to pay $800 cash extra if you do."

The salesman went to ask the manager, and after a few moments came back and said that it could be done and ready by tomorrow. "Great," replied the snail, and left.

The next day the snail returned, signed all the documents, checked out all the snail icons and the letter 'S', then happily paid the money.

As he was about to drive off, the salesman asked, "Do you mind telling me why you wanted the icon and letter changes?"

"Not at all," replied the snail. "When I drive by, everyone will say, 'Look at that S-car go.' "

First Impression

A fossil specialist was making a rubber mold of a special, intricate fossil. He poured the liquid onto the specimen and let it set.

Several hours later, he very carefully and delicately removed the rubber mold. He then made a plaster mix and poured it into the mold and waited for the plaster to harden. When it did, he carefully peeled back the rubber mold, and then examined the casting.

He was not pleased. "I do not understand," he said to his assistant. "I always make a good first impression."

Zapata

Many years ago, at this time of year, there was born a son to a rebel leader in Mexico. The people celebrated because they wanted to hear ZAPATA of little FETES.

Done by Friday

How often have you had someone say to you, "Oh, I will have it to you by Friday!" or "I will have it done by Friday at the latest!" and so on? They are lying.

The best records show that the only person who got everything done and ready by Friday was Robinson Crusoe.

Sausages

A rural farmer of German ancestry with relatives in a nearby city promised the relatives that he would send them some fresh, hand-made sausages from pigs raised on his farm.

The weeks went by, but no sausages showed up, so the city relatives gave the farmer a call to say that the package of sausages had not yet arrived.

He told them, "Don't worry. The wurst is yet to come!"

She Sells

A couple lived near the ocean and used to walk the beach a lot. One summer they noticed a girl who was at the beach almost every day. She wasn't unusual, nor was the travel bag she carried, except for one thing: she would approach people who were sitting on the beach, glance around furtively, then speak to them.

Generally people would respond negatively, and she would wander off; but occasionally someone would nod and there would be a quick exchange of money and something she carried in her bag.

The couple assumed she was selling drugs and debated calling the cops, but since they didn't know for sure, they just continued to watch her. After a couple of weeks the wife said, "Honey, have you ever noticed that she goes only to people with boom boxes and other electronic devices?" He hadn't, and said so!

Then she said, "Tomorrow I want you to get a towel and our big radio and go lie out on the beach. Then we can find out what she's really doing." The plan went off without a hitch, and the wife was almost hopping up and down with anticipation when she saw the girl talk to her husband and then leave. The man then walked up the beach and met his wife at the road.

"Well, is she selling drugs?" she asked excitedly.

"No, she's not," he said, enjoying this probably more than he should have.

"Well, what is it then? What does she do?" his wife fairly shrieked.

The man grinned and said, "She sells batteries."

"Batteries?" cried his wife.

"Yes . . . ," he replied.. . ."she sells C cells by the sea shore."

Silent Letters

Many words used in English have silent letters, for example, "know, honest and knife" to name but a few. Now consider those words that have the silent letter "p", for example the words "pneumonia; psychiatrist; corps; and receipt". There are more words with a silent "p"; however, none of these matches the silent "p" in swimming.

Succeed

Farmer Jones had huge fields of poppies. He supplied not only bakeries with poppy seeds, but also many seed sellers, who packaged them for the public.

Demand was great, and at first he was able to supply all. But as the demand grew, he knew that some would have to be cut from his purchaser lists, and he knew that there was no way he could supply new markets.

As he sat there trying to figure out what to do, he realized as he watched the shaking machines separating the seeds from the poppy seed heads that almost half of the poppy seeds never reached the sacks. Poppy seeds are very small, and in the small currents of air between the separating machines and the sacks, the seeds were spurting into the air. They then fell to the floor, but as there were large cracks between the floor boards, the seeds didn't pile up, and the shaking of the machines caused the seeds to fall between the cracks.

He tried sucking them up with his shop-vac, but that got only a few. Despairing, he started to cry. Friends found him crying hard. He explained the problem to them. They cut holes in a few of the boards, and used huge, powerful vacuums to try to suck up the seeds. In short order, they found that the seeds were being sucked up with the sandy loam under the floor boards, and there was no way to separate the seeds from the loam without germinating the seeds. Farmer Jones started crying again.

This is the origin of the old saying, "If at first you don't suck seeds, cry, cry, again."

Tramp and His Holiday

There was this tramp. One cold winter's morning he was walking along a country road, when he heard a cry for help from a nearby lake.

Without a moment's hesitation he ran out onto the ice and slipped and slid over to a little girl. He managed to pull her out without breaking the ice further and carried her back to the road. He took off his coat and wrapped her in it, then began looking for a car to flag down.

Coincidentally the father drives up. "How can I ever thank you, sir?" he asks after putting his daughter into the warmth of the limo. "Just name your price - I'm a wealthy man."

"Ah, well..," stammers the tramp, "... uh, I'm a little short of cash, perhaps you could help me out."

"Oh dear," says the father, "I don't carry much cash with me, I have only ten pounds - but come home with me and I'll get more from the safe."

"No! No!" says the tramp, "Why ten pounds is more money than I've seen in my whole life - that'll be plenty."

"Ten pounds," thinks the tramp, "I'm rich! I'm rich!" and off he goes to the town to buy himself a holiday.

He finds a travel agent, walks in - much to the disgust of the staff - and goes up to the desk. "I'll have one holiday please!"

"Ahem, which holiday would sir like?" asked the girl at the desk, forcing a smile.

"Oh, any holiday I don't mind, anything up to ten pounds," replies the tramp.

"TEN POUNDS! You'll NEVER get a holiday for ten pounds," says the girl incredulously.

She goes into the back of the shop, and searches in the deepest, dustiest filing drawers she can find. There - to her amazement - she finds an old file.

"Well you'll never believe it," she says to the tramp, back in the shop. "I've got you a holiday – it's a super-duper, ultra-hyper, mega-economy class round-the-world cruise - and it costs ten pounds."

"Yippee!" exclaims the tramp, "I'll take it!"

A few days later he arrives at the port, and there in the dock is the most beautiful, most elaborately decorated, most expensive looking ocean-going liner he has ever seen.

"Get off my ship, ye dirty bum!" shouts a voice, as an irate captain storms down the gangplank and kicks the tramp down onto the dockside.

"But I've got my ticket!" responds the tramp, "Super-duper, ultra-hyper, mega-economy class, and I want on!"

"Well, okay," says the captain. "But you can't come on just now. I don't want my first-class passengers seeing you. Come back at midnight when it's dark and I'll let you on then."

So the tramp finds a quiet spot among some cargo cases on the dockside, and he falls asleep.

"Psst," says a voice, waking him with a start. It was the captain.

"Hurry up, it's midnight, let's get you to your cabin." The tramp toddles after the captain, along the dockside, up the gangway, and onto the ship - and what a ship!

First they went down through the first class level: Oriental carpets – 6-inch pile. There is a genuine Rembrandt on every wall. Leave your shoes outside for cleaning, and the steward brings a new pair. There was 24-carat gold trim everywhere.

Then the second class: As above, but perhaps the carpets were only 3 inches deep, and so on...

Third, Fourth and Fifth class, down past the casinos, and the ballrooms, down through the crew's quarters, down through the galleys, and the engine rooms, until finally, at the lowest point in the ship, against the very hull, the captain opens a watertight door into a tiny seven foot by four foot cabin, with a hammock, a bedside table, and an alarm clock.

"Sheer luxury!" exclaimed the tramp, "A room of my very own."

"I'm glad you like it," replies the captain, "But there is one more thing . . . your class of ticket allows you to use the facilities of the ship only at night -- when all the other passengers are asleep. So that's what the alarm clock is for. Enjoy your cruise."

Well the cruise began, and the tramp had a whale of a time. Sleeping by day, and up on deck at night - he loved it. One-man-tennis, clay pigeon shooting, more food than he'd ever seen...

Then one morning, a week or so into the cruise, the tramp decided he'd have a go on the diving board of the pool. He had just enough time for one dive before he had to go below.

He climbed up the ladder, stepped onto the board tip, bounced, and dived...

... and what a dive...!

Perfectly poised in the air, he hit the water without so much as a ripple.

Now unknown to him, the captain - who'd grown rather fond of the poor old tramp - was standing watching this.

"That was amazing!" exclaimed the captain, "Where did you learn to dive like that?"

"Um, well I've never actually dived before," replied the tramp.

"Well, that's incredible!" says the captain, "I've never seen..." He broke off. "Hey, I've got an idea," he started again. "How would you like to train a bit, and we'll put on a show for the other passengers. I'll pay you, and you can then afford to go first class!"

"It's a deal!" says our man. For the next three weeks the tramp practices like he's never practiced before. Back-flips, front-flips, triple-back sideways axel dives, you name it he tried it.

Then one morning the captain comes to talk. "Okay, I'd like you to stay in your cabin for the next two days. We're going to erect a high diving board for you."

"Okay," agreed the tramp.

Two days passed, and the big day arrived. The ship was humming with excitement. Everyone wanted to see the mystery diver. The captain had provided the tramp with a new pair of swimming trunks, and he wore these as he stepped out onto the sun-beaten deck. There were gasps of astonishment from the crowd, and a hushed awe. Higher than the eye could see, towering up and up, he rose up a slender column of metal.

"Well, tramp," said the captain, shaking his hand, "Let's see what you can do." And with that the captain handed him a walkie-talkie. And the tramp began to climb...

up and up...

below him the ship grew smaller...

on and on...

past a solitary albatross...

and still higher...

till the ship was but a speck on the ocean below...

and on still further...

till the ocean grew dim...

and the earth itself...

began to shrink...

past our moon...

and on...

and Mars...

and on...

higher, and higher...

through the asteroid belt...

and on and on towards the diving board...

past the outer planets, until...

on the outermost reaches of the Solar System...

he reached the board.

He climbed on top and radioed the captain...

and then...

he jumped.

Slowly at first,

but speeding up,

faster, and faster,

speeding past Pluto,

and the other outer planets,

through the asteroid belt,

past Mars,

and the moon,

faster,

and faster,

faster - ever faster,

and by now the earth was growing large in the distance, the oceans and land masses grew clear,

faster, and faster,

past the albatross,

double-back somersault,

and he could see the ship, tiny in the distance, hurtling down now, he posed, ready for the final 500 feet,

Down on the ship the crew strained their necks,

"I CAN SEE HIM!" yelled a passenger, "LOOK!!!"

The tramp streaked down towards the pool, did a last triple flip, and dove...

NOT A RIPPLE ON THE SURFACE!

DOWN THROUGH THE WATER!

SMASHED THROUGH THE POOL BOTTOM!

DOWN THROUGH THE FIRST DECK!

SMASHING THROUGH THE SECOND!

DOWN!

DOWN!

THROUGH THE CREW'S QUARTERS!

THROUGH THE ENGINE ROOMS!

SMASHING THROUGH TO HIS OWN LITTLE CABIN!

AND DOWN THROUGH THE DOUBLE-STRENGTH STEEL HULL OF THE SHIP!

STILL DOWN...!

DEEPER,

DEEPER INTO THE MURKY DEPTHS,

TILL.........

SMASH!

Into the sea bed, sinking a 37-foot shaft in the process.

Desperate for air he struggled out of the shaft, his lungs bursting, he swam frantically for the surface.

Up and up, desperate, gasping...

Out of the water, up the ladder onto the deck of the ship he goes, into a throng wild with acclaim.

"HERO!" "WONDERFUL!" "AMAZING!" "GOOD SHOW THAT!"

And handing him a heated towel the captain spoke, as a hush fell over the crowd.

"Well tramp, I have NEVER seen anything like that, EVER. That was the most *STUPENDOUS* piece of diving I have ever seen."

The tramp blushed.

The captain went on, "But tell me, most amazing of all is how you survived smashing through this boat after you dived - how did you do it."

And the tramp looked at the captain, and then at the crowd, and replied modestly: "Well you see...

I'm a just poor tramp...

So you must understand...

I've been through many a hard ship in my life."

Word Play

When a clock is hungry, it goes back four seconds.

Intellectual Puns

A Canadian lass was in Glasgow when she saw a Scot striding towards her, his kilt swaying. She asked him, "Is anything ever worn under the kilt?" His reply, "Nay, Lassie, it's always in fine working order.."

A 3-legged dog walks into an old west saloon, slides up to the bar and announces, "I'm looking for the man who shot my paw."

Did you hear about the Buddhist who went to the dentist, and refused to take Novocain? He wanted to transcend dental medication.

A women has twins, gives them up for adoption. One goes to an Egyptian family and is named "Ahmal" The other is sent to a Spanish family and is named "Juan". Years later, Juan sends his birth mother a picture of himself. Upon

154

receiving the picture, she tells her husband she wishes she also had a picture of Ahmal. He replies, "They're twins for Pete sake!! If you've seen Juan, you've seen Ahmal!!"

Mahatma Gandhi, as you know, walked barefoot his whole life, which created an impressive set of calluses on his feet. He also ate very little, which made him frail, and with his odd diet, he suffered from very bad breath. This made him ...what?: A super-calloused fragile mystic hexed by halitosis.

Two hats were hanging on a hat rack in the hallway. One hat said to the other, "You stay here while I go on ahead.

Atheism is a non-prophet organization. Remember, do not join dangerous cults: practice safe sects.

A small boy swallowed some coins and was taken to a hospital. His grandmother phoned to ask how he is. A nurse replied, "No change yet."

I wondered why the baseball kept on getting bigger and bigger. Then it hit me.

Edmonton Journal Headline Puns

A knack for nitpicking leads to successful delousing business.

The Edmonton Journal, 1 October 2008, page B1.

Open water puts Arctic trek on ice.

The Edmonton Journal, 14 February 2010, page A5.

Earthy Salacious Puns: Read At Your Own Risk

Earthy, Mostly One-Liners

Dancing cheek-to-cheek is really a form of floor play.

Condoms should be used on every conceivable occasion.

A hole has been found in the nudist camp wall. The police are looking into it.

The best fly control is to keep the zipper up all the time.

A man needs a mistress just to break the monogamy.

Is a book on voyeurism a peeping tome?

Banning the bra was a big flop.

Propaganda: a gentlemanly goose.

Even if you are on the right track, you'll be run over if you just sit there.

There was a lady news anchor who, after it was supposed to have snowed and didn't, turned to the weatherman and asked, "So, Bob, where's that 8 inches you promised me last night?"

He does not have a BEER GUT – He has developed a LIQUID GRAIN STORAGE FACILITY.

After the Christening

After the christening of his baby brother in church, little Johnny sobbed all the way home in the car. His father asked him three times what was wrong. Finally he replied, "That priest said he wanted us to be brought up in a Christian home, but I want to stay with you guys.

What a Coincidence

A man sat at a local bar and said, "This is a very special day I'm celebrating."

"What a coincidence," said the woman next to him. "What are you celebrating?"

"I'm a chicken farmer, and for years, all my hens were infertile. But today they're finally all fertile."

"What a coincidence," the woman said. "My husband and I have been trying to have a child for several years. Today, my gynecologist told me that I'm pregnant! How did your chickens become fertile?" He replied, "I switched cocks."

"What a coincidence," she said.

Two Vampires

Two vampires wanted to go out to eat, but were having a little trouble deciding where to go. They were a little tired of the local food in Transylvania and wanted something a little more exotic.

After some discussion, they decided to go to Italy because they had heard that Italian food was really good. So off they went to Italy and ended up in Venice. On a bridge over one of the canals, they hid in the shadows and waited for dinner. A few minutes later they noticed a young couple walking their way. As they neared, the vampires made their move. Each vampire grabbed a person, sucked each dry, and tossed the bodies into the canal below.

The vampires were extremely pleased with their meal and decided to have seconds. Another young couple approached a few minutes later and suffered the same fate as the first - sucked dry and tossed into the canal below. The vampires decided that they had had a marvelous dinner, but that it was time to head back home. As they started to walk away, they began to hear someone singing. They were puzzled because no one else was on the bridge. As they listened, they realized that it was coming from the canal. They looked over the rail and saw a big alligator in the water under the bridge, feasting on the bodies. They listened as the alligator sang:

You don't know what the alligator sang, do you?

"Drained wops keep falling on my head...".

Trade, No-Cash Deal

A woman enters a tattoo parlor and requests a tattoo. She also offers to pay, not in cash, but by letting the artist feel her breasts. Your assignment, if you choose to accept it, is to describe this offer in the tersest possible terms.

Answer: Tit for tat. (GRN)

Birds at Play

Today, I watched some birds at play near my dentist's office. His hygienist kept telling me to swallow, until I suggested that she ought to be trying to lure a different bird.

How to get to Heaven!

Queen Elizabeth and Dolly Parton die on the same day, and they both go before the angel to find out if they'll be admitted to Heaven. Unfortunately, there's only one space left that day, so the angel must decide which of them gets in.

The angel asks Dolly if there's a particular reason why she should go to Heaven, whereupon she takes off her top and says, "Look at these. They're the most perfect breasts God ever created, and I'm sure it will please God to be able to see them every day, for eternity."

The angel thanks Dolly, and asks Her Majesty the same question. The Queen takes a bottle of Perrier out of her purse, shakes it up, and gargles. Then, she spits into the toilet, and pulls the lever. The angel says, "OK, your Majesty, you may go in."

Dolly is outraged and asks, "What was that all about? I show you two of God's own perfect creations, and you turn me down. She simply gargles and she gets in. Would you explain that to me?"

"Sorry, Dolly," says the angel, "but even in Heaven, a royal flush beats a pair, no matter how big they are!

One Word Or Two Words?

An elderly couple had been dating for some time. Finally they decided it was time for marriage. Before the wedding, they went out to dinner and had a long conversation regarding how their marriage might work.

They discussed finances, living arrangements, and so on. Finally the old gentleman decided it was time to broach the subject of their physical relationship.

"How do you feel about sex?" he asked, rather trustingly.

"Well," she says, responding very carefully, "I'd have to say I would like it infrequently."

The old gentleman sat quietly for a moment.

Then looking over his glasses, looked her in the eye casually, and asked, "Was that one word or two words?"

Lawyer Talk

A man walked into a bar. He saw a good-looking, smartly dressed woman perched on a barstool.

He walked up to her and said, "Hi there, good looking. How is it going?"

She turned around, faced him, looked him straight in the eye and said,

"Listen, 'I'll screw anybody, anytime, anywhere, your place, my place. It doesn't matter. I've been doing it ever since I got out of college. I just flat out love it!"

He said, "No kidding? I'm a lawyer, too! What firm are you with?"

The Scotsman at a Baseball Game

A Scotsman was at a baseball game. It was the first time he had ever seen the sport, so he sat quietly. The first batter approached the plate, took a few swings, and then hit a double. Everyone was on their feet screaming, "Run, Run!"

This happened two more times with a single and a triple. The Scot was now excited and ready to get into the game. The next batter came up and four balls went by. The umpire called, "Walk", and the batter started on a slow trot to first. The Scot, extremely excited now, stood up and screamed, "R-R-Run, ye bastard, rrrrun!"

Everyone around him started laughing, so the Scot, extremely embarrassed, sat back down. The fan sitting next to the Scot noticed the embarrassment, so he leaned over and explained, "He can't run because he's got four balls."

The Scot stood up immediately and screamed, "Walk with pride, man! Walk with pride!"

No Bull

Two cows are standing next to each other in a field, Daisy says to Dolly, "I was artificially inseminated this morning." "I don't believe you," says Dolly. "It's true, no bull!" exclaims Daisy.

Meredith Willson's Memoirs

Meredith Willson's memoirs reveal that he came into possession of an illicit photograph of Deanna Durbin and Gary Cooper going at it. Willson says it inspired one of his songs,

"Gary in Deanna."

Blondes Have More Fun

A group of very attractive young female city employees discovered they could nicely supplement their income by moonlighting as call girls.

One of the girls discovered she was more successful as a blonde after having her hair bleached. She convinced the others that the old saying, "Blondes have more fun," is true.

The ladies became so popular that they were able to charge exorbitant rates. They even charged their taxi fares to the johns they served.

When hard times hit and the market got soft, they needed a bigger come-on. Some of them understood the economic law of supply and demand, so decided to lower their rates. They decided not to include taxi fares in the fees they charged their customers.

They have since become known as: The taxi-free municipal blondes.

Decorum

The bride-to-be was advised by the marriage counsellor to never disrobe completely in front of her husband when retiring for decorum's sake.

One night, six weeks after the wedding, the husband said to his bride, "Is there any insanity in your family?"

"Why, no," she said. "Why do you ask?"

"I was merely wondering," he asked, "why you haven't taken your hat off since we've been married?"

One - Knight Stand

Several of the Knights of the Round Table were returning from a long journey. They were tired and very thirsty. They were delighted when they found a roadside stand.

They all dismounted, and the first to the stand was served a long, cold mug of mead. However, when the second and third asked for the same drink, the owner said, "Sorry, I cannot serve you!"

Somewhat insulted, the second asked, "And why not?"

"Well, you see," said the owner, "This is a one-Knight stand."

Adult Twists To Childrens' Stories

Cinderella

Cinderella wants to go to the ball, but her wicked step-mother won't let her. As Cinderella sits crying in the garden, her fairy godmother appears, and promises to provide Cinderella with everything she needs to go to the ball, but only on two conditions.

"First, you must wear a diaphragm." Cinderella agrees.

"What's the second condition?" "You must be home by 2 a.m. Any later, and your diaphragm will turn into a pumpkin."

Cinderella agrees to be home by 2 a.m. The appointed hour comes and goes, and Cinderella doesn't show up. Finally, at 5 a.m., Cinderella shows up, looking lovestruck and *very* satisfied.

"Where have you been?" demands the Fairy Godmother. "Your diaphragm was supposed to turn into a pumpkin three hours ago!!!"

"I met a prince, Fairy Godmother. He took care of everything."

"I know of no prince with that kind of power! Tell me his name!"

"I can't remember, exactly . . . . it's Peter Peter, something or other...."

Snow White's Problem

Snow White saw Pinocchio walking through the woods, so she ran up behind him, knocked him flat on his back, and then sat on his face crying, "Lie to me! Lie to me!"

Splinters and Sandpaper

Pinocchio had a human girlfriend who would sometimes complain about splinters when they were having sex. Pinocchio, therefore, went to visit Gepetto to see if he could help. Gepetto suggested he try a little sandpaper wherever indicated, and Pinocchio skipped away enlightened. A couple of weeks later, Gepetto saw Pinocchio bouncing happily through the town and asked him, "How's the girlfriend?"

Pinocchio replied, "Who needs a girlfriend?"

Can You Figure This Out?

Snow White and the Seven Dwarfs are roaming in the forest when they come to a lake. The water is enticing, so Snow White decides to take a bath. She tells the Dwarfs to turn around while she is taking a bath in the lake.

The Dwarfs protest vehemently because they want to take a bath, too. Snow White relents and says, "When I get into the water and you hear the splash, you can turn around."

Snow White undresses and as she is about to jump into the water, at that very same moment, she is startled by a frog, which jumps into the water before she can.

The moment the Dwarfs hear the SPLASH, they turn around and see Snow White standing NAKED.

Now, given that this incident is an idea for a TV ad, what product is being advertised?

SEVEN UP!

Adult, Earthy Puns

Boston Fish Market

Two old biddies are in Boston's fish market on Friday. One said to the other, "I come to town every Friday to get scrod!"

"I do, too," replied the other. "But I didn't know that it had a past tense.

Crazy Divorce

Mickey Mouse and Minnie Mouse were in divorce court and the judge said to Mickey,

"You say here that your wife is crazy."

Mickey replied, "I didn't say she is crazy. I said she is f**king Goofy."

Love Under Glass

A man is dining in a fancy restaurant and there is a gorgeous redhead sitting at the next table. He has been checking her out since he sat down, but lacks the nerve to talk with her.

Suddenly she sneezes, and her glass eye pops out, flying from its socket towards the man.

He reflexively reaches out, grabs it out of the air, and hands it back to her.

"Oh my, I am so sorry," the woman says as she pops her eye back in place.

"Let me buy your dinner to make it up to you," she says.

They enjoy a wonderful dinner together, and afterwards they go to the theater followed by drinks. They talk, they laugh, she shares her deepest dreams, and he shares his. She listens.

After paying for everything, she asks him if he would like to come to her place for a nightcap and stay for breakfast.

They had a wonderful, wonderful time.

The next morning, she cooks a gourmet meal with all the trimmings.

The guy is amazed!! Everything had been SO incredible!!!!

"You know," he said, "you are the perfect woman. Are you this nice to every guy you meet? "

"No," she replies, "you just happened to catch my eye."

Bleach Blonde

Two women were having lunch together, and discussing the merits of cosmetic surgery. The first woman says, "I need to be honest with you. I'm getting a boob job!"

The second woman says, "Oh, that's nothing. I'm thinking of having my asshole bleached!"

To which the first replies, "Whoa...I just can't picture your husband as a blonde!"

Clerical Book

Several clergy have co-authored a new book. It is titled:

"Ministers Do More Than Lay People."

Following Instructions

Aunt Annie was in her 80s, and much admired for her sweetness and kindness to all. The pastor came to call one afternoon, and she welcomed him into her Victorian parlor. She invited him to have a seat while she prepared a little tea.

As he sat facing her old pump organ, the young minister noticed a cut glass bowl sitting on top of it, filled with water. In the water was floating, of all things...a condom.

Imagine his shock and surprise. Imagine his curiosity! Surely Aunt Annie had flipped or something...!

But he certainly couldn't mention the strange sight in her parlor. When she returned with tea and cookies, they began to chat. The pastor tried to stifle his curiosity about the bowl of water and its strange floater, but soon it got the better of him, and he could resist no longer.

"Aunt Annie," he asked, "I wonder if you could tell me about this?" (he pointed to the bowl)

"Oh, yes," she replied, "isn't it wonderful? I was walking downtown last fall, and I found this little package. The directions said to put it on the organ, keep it wet, and it would prevent disease. And you know...I haven't had a cold all winter!"

The Preacher's Mule

A preacher decided to try to raise a little extra money for his small congregation. He heard that money could be made by racing horses, so he went to the local auction

sales. He found that the only thing he could was a mule. Having faith, he purchased it and took it home.

Using that same faith, he entered the mule in the local horse race. Much to everyone's surprise, it came in third. Next week, when the local racing sheet came out, the lead headline read,

"PREACHER'S ASS SHOWS."

Encouraged by the results of the first race, the preacher entered the mule in a second race. This time the mule won. The lead headline read, "PREACHER'S ASS OUT IN FRONT."

Someone showed these headlines to the Bishop. Understandably, he did not appreciate the type of attention the headlines implied, so the Bishop told the preacher to quit racing the mule. The lead headline read, "BISHOP SCRATCHES PREACHER'S ASS."

When the Bishop saw this headline, he ordered the preacher to get rid of the mule. The preacher gave it to a local nun. Next week, the racing sheet headline came out with, "NUN HAS BEST ASS IN TOWN."

When the Bishop saw that headline, he fainted, he ordered the nun to get rid of the mule. She sold the mule to a travelling merchant for $10. Next week the racing sheet headline read,

"NUN PEDDLES ASS FOR TEN DOLLARS."

Jewish Divorce

A New York judge is presiding over the divorce proceedings of a Jewish couple. When the final papers have been signed and the divorce is complete, the woman thanks the judge and says, "Now I have to arrange for a GHET."

The judge inquires what she means by a "Ghet". So, the woman explains that a Ghet is a religious ceremony required under the Jewish religion in order to receive a divorce recognized by the Jewish faith.

The judge asks, "You mean a religious ceremony like a Bris?" (Circumcision)

She replies, "Yes, very similar, only in this case you get rid of the entire prick!"

No Supper

The proctologist phoned his wife and told her he wouldn't be home for supper because he was: working late at the orifice. (RCC)

Monica's Tonsils

A surgeon went to check on his very famous patient after an operation. She was awake, so he examined her thoroughly and told her that she could expect a complete recovery.

She asked him, "How long will it be before I can resume a normal sex life again, Doctor?"

The surgeon seemed to pause, which alarmed the girl.

"What's the matter, Doctor? I will be all right, won't I?"

He replied, "Yes, you'll be fine, Miss Lewinsky. It's just that no one has ever asked me that after having their tonsils out."

Full Noodle

Two patrons in a pasta restaurant got into a heated argument. One lost his temper and made so bold as to dump an entire bowl of spaghetti onto his opponent, covering him from head to toe. He was promptly arrested for displaying--what?--in a public place.

Answer: Full noodle effrontery. (RCC)

More Clinton

After much arguing and deliberation, historians this week have come up with a phrase to describe the Clinton Era. It will be called: SEX BETWEEN THE BUSHES.

The Center for Disease Control in Atlanta announced that Clinton has proven that you can get sex from Aides.

Gennifer Flowers was asked if her relationship with Clinton was anything like that of Monica Lewinski's. She replied, "Close, but no cigar."

The FBI has coined a technical term for the stains found on Monica's dress: "Presidue."

Clinton now recruits interns from just four colleges: Moorhead, Oral Roberts, Ball State and Brigham Young.

Little Hookers

Two diminutive prostitutes used to stow away on helicopters taking men into battle, servicing them on the flight. What were they called?

The Little Chopper Whores.

First-Nation's Man with One Testicle

There once was a First-Nation's man whose given name was "Onestone". He was so named because he had only one testicle. He hated that name, and asked everyone not to call him "Onestone".

After years and years of torment, Onestone finally cracked and said, "If anyone calls me 'Onestone' again, I will kill him or her!" The word got around, and nobody called him that any more.

Then one day a young woman named Blue Bird forgot and said, "Good morning, Onestone." He jumped up, grabbed her, and took her deep into the forest where he made love to her all day and all night. He made love to her all the next day, until Blue Bird died from exhaustion.

The word got around that Onestone meant what he promised he would do. Years went by and no one dared call him by his given name until a woman named Yellow Bird returned to the village after being away for many years.

Yellow Bird, who was Blue Bird's cousin, was overjoyed when she saw Onestone. She hugged him and said, "Good to see you, Onestone."

Onestone grabbed her, took her deep into the forest, then he made love to her all day, made love to her all night, made love to her all the next day, made love to her all the next night, but Yellow Bird wouldn't die!

The moral is you can't kill two birds with one stone.

Redneck

A fresh-faced lad on the eve of his wedding night asks his mother,

"Mum, why are wedding dresses white?"

The mother looks at her son and replies,

"Son, this shows the world that your bride is pure."

The son thanks his mum, and then seeks his father's opinion.

"Dad, why are wedding dresses white?"

The father looks at his son in surprise and says,

"Son, all household appliances come in white."

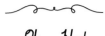

Oh, No!

A middle-aged woman seemed timid as she visited her gynecologist.

"Come now," coaxed the doctor, "you've been seeing me for years! There's nothing you can't tell me."

"This one's kind of strange..." said the woman.

"Let me be the judge of that," the doctor replied.

"Well," said the woman, "Yesterday I went to the bathroom in the morning and I heard a plink-plink in the toilet. When I looked down, the water was full of pennies."

"Mmmm, I see." said the, doctor.

"That afternoon I went again and there were nickels in the bowl."

"Uh huh." the doctor said as he got more and more interested in her story.

"That night," she went on, "there were dimes, and this morning there were quarters! You've got to tell me what's wrong with me!" she implored. "I'm scared out of my wits!"

The gynecologist put a comforting hand on her shoulder. "There is nothing to be frightened about. You're simply going through the change."

Best Evidence Rule

One day in 1984, for the entire fifty minutes of the class, Professor George Nock had me on the "hot seat" in his year-long evidence class. Although he and I had become friends, I sweated bullets the next day when I wore a motorcycle helmet to his class … for protection.

I thought I was safe, but Professor Nock called on me.

"Ms Kogut, what is the doctrine that an original document is superior to a copy?"

"The best evidence rule," I answered.

"And what is the doctrine that holy water is superior to ordinary tap water?"

"Uh?" I responded.

"It's the 'blessed evidence rule,' of course. Now, what's the doctrine that white chicken meat is superior to dark chicken meat?"

"Uh?" I stammered again.

"The breast evidence rule." (MAK)

Nag, Nag, Nag...

A lawyer arrived home late one night after a very tough day of trying to get a stay of execution. His last minute plea for clemency to the governor had failed, and he was feeling worn out and depressed.

As soon as he walked through the door at home, his wife started in on him about:

"What time of night is this to be getting home?"

"Where have you been?"

"Dinner is cold, and I am not reheating it!"

And on, and on, and on....

Too tired and shattered to play his usual role in this familiar ritual, he poured himself a shot of Scotch and headed off for a long, hot soak in the bathtub - pursued by the predictable sarcastic remarks as he dragged himself up the stairs.

While he was running the water into the tub, the Governor's office phoned. The Governor said that her husband's client, George Wright, would not be executed at midnight, but that the sentence had been commuted to life in prison. She said that she would tell him.

Finally realizing what a terrible day he had had, she decided to go upstairs and give him the good news. As she opened the bathroom door, she was greeted by a rear-end view of her husband, bent over, naked, drying his legs and feet.

Sympathetically she said, "They're not hanging Wright tonight, dear!"

He whirled around and screamed, **"For the love of God, woman, don't you ever stop?"**

Decision: Whom to Fire?

Joe had to get rid of one of his staff. He had narrowed it to two people: Debra or Jack. It would be a hard decision to make, as they were equally qualified, and both did excellent work. He finally decided that in the morning whichever one used the water cooler first would have to go.

Debra came in the next morning, hugely hung over after partying all night. As she went to the cooler to get some water and to take an aspirin, the executive approached her and said,

"Debra, I've never done this before, but I have to lay you or Jack off."

Debra replied, "Could you jack off? I have a terrible headache."

New Alloy

It's taken a great deal of courage, some of it Dutch (or, more precisely, Scotch), to come up with the following. Please don't hate me.

Scientists have done the previously thought impossible, by creating a new alloy between organic and inorganic matter. Specifically, it is an alloy of jism and tin. I'm sure you can figure out its name.

Answer: Cum Pewter.

A Dilemma

A man who had been called to testify at the Internal Revenue Service asked his accountant for advice on what to wear. The accountant advised,

"Wear your shabbiest clothing. Let them think you are a pauper."

Then he asked his lawyer the same question, but got the opposite advice,

"Don't let them intimidate you. Wear your most elegant suit and tie."

Confused, the man went to his priest, told him of the conflicting advice, and requested some resolution to the dilemma.

"Let me tell you a story," replied the priest. "A woman, about to be married, asked her mother what to wear on her wedding night." Her mother said, "Wear a heavy, long, flannel nightgown that goes right up to your neck."

But when she asked her best friend, she got conflicting advice. Her friend said, "Wear your most sexy negligee, with a V-neck right down to your navel."

Confused, the man asked, "What does all this have to do with my problem with the IRS?"

"Simple," replied the priest. "It doesn't matter what you wear, you're still going to get screwed."

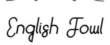

English Fowl

What menu item is a virtual homophone for an alternative moniker for the Drag Queen of Penzance?

Answer: Cornish Game Hen. (GRN)

To keep them on their Toes

At the local monastery, the Head Monk decided to raise the height of the urinals 15 cm. The reason: it was felt that the monks were slacking a bit, and needed something to help keep them on their toes.

Tale of Two Cities

A high-priced hooker had been plying her trade between Edmonton and Calgary for many years, extracting money from oil company executives. The RCMP was aware of her and tried to catch her numerous times. But the problem is that the RCMP jurisdiction does not apply in these two cities. She was eventually caught soliciting by Edmonton an undercover police officer. After her services, she was pleased to give him her business card, for future services of course, which read, "Tail of Two Cities. Do Come Again."

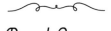

Papal Camera

The Pope was having a shower. Although he was very strict about the Celibacy rules, he occasionally felt the need to exercise the right wrist, and this was one of these occasions.

Just as he reached the Papal Climax, he saw a paparazzi photographer capturing the moment of the holy seed flying through the air. "Hold on a minute," said the Pope. "You can't publish that. You'll destroy the reputation of the Catholic Church."

"This picture is my lottery win," said the photographer. "I'll be financially secure for life."

So, the Pope offered to buy the camera from the photographer, and after lots of negotiation, they eventually arrived at a figure of two million dollars.

The Pope then dried himself off and headed off with his new camera.

He met his housekeeper, who spotted the camera. "That looks like a really good camera," she said. "How much did it cost you?"

"Two million dollars," replied the Pope.

"TWO MILLION DOLLARS!" said the housekeeper, "They must have seen you coming."

Teapot

A guy was fixing a door and found that he needed a new hinge, so he sent his wife to the hardware store.

At the hardware store, while she was waiting for the manager to finish waiting on another customer, she saw a beautiful teapot on a top shelf. When it was her turn, she asked about the price of the teapot. He replied, "It's silver, and it costs $100."

"My goodness, that sure is a lotta money," she exclaimed.

Then she proceeded to describe the hinge that her husband had sent her to buy. The manager went to the back room to find it. From the back room he yelled, "Do you wanna screw for the hinge?" To which she replied, "No, but I will for the teapot!"

Apocryphal Story

I was in bed last night with a blind woman, and she said that I had the biggest penis that she had ever put her hands around.

I replied, "You're pulling my leg."

Service

At one time in my life, I thought I had a handle on the meaning of the word "service". The act of doing things for other people. Then I heard the words "Public Service, Postal Service, Civil Service and others." I became confused about the word "service".

This not what I thought what I thought "service" meant. Then one day, I overheard two farmers talking and one of them mentioned that he was having a bull service a few of his cows.

BINGO! It all came into perspective. Now I understand what all those "service" agencies are doing to us . . . .

Doctor's Equipment

A man went into the proctologist's office for his first exam. The doctor told him to have a seat in the examination room, and that he would be with him in a few minutes. When the man sat down, he began observing the tools. He noticed that there were 3 items on a stand next to the doctor's desk: a tube of K-Y jelly; a pair of rubber gloves; and a bottle of beer.

When the doctor finally came in, the man asked, "Look, doc. I'm a little confused. This is my first exam. I know what the K-Y jelly and what the gloves are for, but can you tell me what the BUD LITE is for?"

At that, the doctor became noticeably upset and flung the door open and yelled to his nurse . . . "Dammit, Helen! My writing's not that bad. I wrote "A BUTT LIGHT!"

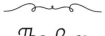

The Cure

Two old folk got married. As they were lying in their wedding suite, staring at the ceiling, the old man says, "I haven't been completely honest with you. I think the world of you, but you are only number two to me. Golf is my first love. It's my hobby, my passion, my first love."

They both stare at the ceiling for a bit longer, and then the old woman says, "While we are baring our souls, I guess I had better tell you that I have been a hooker all my life."

The man jumps out of bed, looks at her for a moment, then says, "Have you tried widening your stance and adjusting your grip?"

Penal Code 288

California Penal Code Section 288 describes various sexual offenses (it really does). Why is it seldom discussed in the legal community?

Answer: It's two gross. (GRN)

Listen!

The Nipol Computer company announced today that it has developed a new computer chip that can store and play high fidelity music in women's breast implants.

The chip will cost between $499 and $699, depending on speaker size.

This is considered to be a major breakthrough because women have always complained that men stare at their breasts and do not listen to them.

Olympic Condoms

A husband said to his wife: "My Olympic condoms have arrived ... I think I'll wear Gold tonight."

And his wife replied: "Why not wear Silver and come second for a change?"

Butter is Better

A man is showering up in a locker room with his buddy when he notices his friend is very well endowed. "Damn, Bob, but you're hung!" Jim exclaims.

"I wasn't always this impressive. I had to work for it."

"What do you mean?" Jim asked.

"Well, every day for the past two years I've spent an hour each night rubbing it with butter. I know it sounds crazy but it actually made it grow 4 inches! You should try it."

Jim agrees and the two say good bye.

A few months later the two are in the same locker room, and Bob asks Jim how his situation was. Jim replied, " I did what you said, Bob, but I've actually gotten smaller!- - I lost two inches already!"

"Did you do everything I told you? You spent an hour each day with butter?"

"Well, I was out of butter, so I've been using Crisco."

"Crisco?" Bob exclaimed, "Dammit, Jim, Crisco's shortening!"

Rye Bread

Two old guys, one 80 and the other 87, were sitting on their usual park bench one morning.

The 87-year-old man had just finished his morning jog and wasn't even huffing. His 80-year-old friend was amazed at his friend's stamina and asked him what he did to have so much energy.

The 87-year-old replied, "Well, I eat rye bread every day. It keeps my energy level high, and I have great stamina with the ladies."

So, on his way home, the 80-year-old stopped in at the bakery. As he was looking around, a lady asked if he needed any help.

He asked, "Do you have any rye bread?"

She replied, "Yes, we do. We have a whole shelf of it. How much would you like?"

He said, "I want 5 loaves, please."

She replied, "My goodness! 5 loaves? By the time you get to the third one, it'll be hard."

He muttered, "I can't believe it. Everyone knows about this but me!"

Letter to the Editor

A dear friend of mine had the following letter printed in the San Francisco Chronicle:

> *Editor -- They may have gone too far this time. I had gotten grudgingly used to hearing "faux" overused as an adjective in English. I could tolerate "faux windows" and a "faux wall covering" and so forth. Monday night, however, as I walked past the TV, the Home Improvement Channel was using "faux" as a verb!*
>
> *The decorators were uttering such monstrosities as, "Let's faux that décor" and "Mirrors will enable us to faux the dimensions of this space," etc. I wonder what the forms of the verb are. Would I say, "They have fauxed (fauxn?) the wallpaper?" "She is fauxing the surface?" The whole thing makes me want to faux up.*
>
> *William F. Tamerlane*
> *San Ramon*

Herewith my reply:

> Excellent letter! Congratulations!
>
> Exploring the matter further, could a cuckold be a faux pa?
>
> Using the word as a noun, "who goes there, friend or faux?"

Considering improper pronunciations, faux populi faux dei.

Do you ever watch Faux News Channel?

Hope we never wind up in an old faux home. (GRN)

Cutting the Grass

One Saturday afternoon, a man was sitting in his lawn chair drinking beer and watching his wife mow the lawn.

A neighbor lady was so outraged. She came over and shouted at the man, "You should be hung!"

To which he calmly replied, "I am, and that's why she cuts the grass!"

On Being a Scotsman

A Scottish Jew who had worked hard all his life in Edinburgh decided that he would like to enjoy life a little, so he went to the exclusive St Andrews Club. He was told on applying that his application would have to be approved by the Membership Board and that he would receive their decision in a couple of days.

Two days later he was told that his application was refused. He went to the club and asked why. He was asked, "You're Jewish, aren't you?"

"Aye," he answered, "but I'm as Scottish as you are Jock."

"Well, you understand that we wear nothing under our kilts."

"Aye, I know that."

"And, being Jewish, you must be circumcised."

"Aye, I am that."

"Well, the board decided that they could not tolerate a circumcised man parading around with us."

"Och, away with ye man," the Jew cried. "I know I need to be a Protestant to march in the Orangeman's Parade, and a Catholic to belong to the Knights of Columbus, but this is the first time I've heard that a man has to be a complete prick to be a Scotsman!"

Premature

A young couple, on the brink of divorce, visits a marriage counsellor. The counsellor asks the wife, "What's the problem?"

She responds, "My husband suffers from premature ejaculation."

The counsellor turns to her husband and inquires, "Is that true?"

The husband replies, "Well not exactly, she's the one who suffers, not I."

Law to Limerick

Rex Collings had been a brilliant law student and professor at Berkeley. At some point, however, he deteriorated mentally. He frequently made comments in class on students' breast or penile size. But the students had the last word. The following graffito was found on a law school men's room wall:

> *There was a professor named Rex,*
> *Who was small in the organs of sex.*
> *When charged with exposure,*
> *He pled, with composure:*
> *De minimus non curat lex.* (GRN)

Origin of Shakespearean Play Names

Nocturnal Emission: Midsummer Night's Dream.

Miscarriage: Love's Labor Lost.

75 mm: Much Ado About Nothing.

150 mm: As You Like It.

200 mm and more: Taming of the Shrew.

A Different Perspective

Superman had it, and so do a few others. People with apodyopsis have a very different, interesting and perceptive view of others.

Special Therapy

A woman who suffered from occasional bouts of depression visited her doctor for advice. He recommended that she go to a group therapy session. That evening, she told her father that she was going out to attend the therapy session recommended by her doctor.

When she came home several hours later, she literally bounced into the house, and she had a great big smile on her face. Her father was impressed, but he didn't have to say anything. Her disposition told it all, and she said to her dad, "That was an amazing grope therapy session. I am going again!"

The Heimlich Maneuver

Two cowboys from One-Four, Alberta, walked into a roadhouse to wash the trail dust from their throats. They were standing at the bar, drinking their beers and talking quietly.

Suddenly a woman at a nearby table, who has been eating a sandwich, began to cough. After a few seconds, it became apparent that she is in real distress, so the cowboys turn to look at her.

"Can ya swaller?" asks one of the cowboys. The woman shakes her head "No!".

"Can ya breathe?" asks the other.

The woman again shakes her head "No" and starts turning a bit blue.

The first cowboy walks over to her, lifts up the back of her skirt, yanks down her panties, and slowly runs his tongue from the back of her thigh up to the small of her back. This shocks the woman into a violent spasm, and as the obstruction flies out of her mouth, she begins to breathe again.

The cowboy walks back to the bar and takes a drink from his beer. His buddy says, "Ya know, I'd heard of that there Hind Lick Maneuver, but I never seen anybody do it."

The Bald Eagle

The Bald Eagle is the greatest and most venerated icon of the United States of America. Its image, one way or another (photo, drawing, metal casting, plaque, letterhead, etc.) is found on most U.S.A. federal government material. It is often portrayed with a cluster of arrows in each set of claws.

It was not discovered until late April 1998 that this name for this bird is in error. A BioSciences student from the Alberta Northern Alberta Institute of Technology (NAIT), during the Spring Field Course, determined that the correct common name for this species of bird is Balled Eagle.

Thanks so much Lucy! So nice you remember Robin

Robin Leech
& Lorie J. Taylor Leech

Lorie Hay & Leech.

The Author & Illustrator

Robin Leech, P.Biol., graduated from UBC (1963) in Botany and Zoology with a minor in English. His MSc (1965) and PhD (1971) were taken at the U of Alberta, Edmonton; NRC post-doc fellowship in Ottawa. Both graduate degrees were on spider classification and biogeography. By 19, he had been to the Firth River near the Yukon coast. Undergrad studies were not continuous, as they were interrupted by an expedition to Africa, one to Indochina (bubonic plague research), and then two trips to Antarctica. He is a Charter Member of the American Arachnological Society, and serves on its Common

Names Committee. He served for almost 40 years as an Associate Editor of The Entomological Society of Canada. He has two children from a previous marriage, and three grandchildren. His wife Lorie J. Taylor Leech is a fine artist and illustrator, and an educator (BGS; BEd.), who has come to enjoy working with and studying spiders. He is a Charter Member and Life Member of the Alberta Society of Professional Biologists, and from 2002 to 2009 was its Executive Director. He taught many different courses in Biological Sciences at the Northern Alberta Institute of Technology, starting in 1984 and retiring from there in 2002. He has 143 publications, mostly on spiders and arthropods, but also on such diverse subjects as reloading firearms cartridges and Canadian-made binoculars. For hobbies he repairs the older mechanical watches, does close-up photography, and teaches firearms safety courses.

Index

Reader Caution: There are Earthy Puns listed below. These are indented from the left margin, and are on pages 156 onward. Read at your own risk.

205

207